# A DREAM COME TRUE

FOSTERING THROUGH THE EYES OF A CHILD | VOLUME 4

# A DREAM COME TRUE

**LIFE BEYOND THE HORIZON**

## DESMOND TOMLINSON

**MANGIFERA BLOOM**

Port St Lucie

Copyright © 2020 Desmond Tomlinson
All rights reserved.

Published by Mangifera Bloom, Port St Lucie

All rights reserved. No part of this book may be reproduced, stored, or transmitted by any means—whether auditory, graphic, mechanical, or electronic—without written permission of the publisher except in the case of brief excerpts used in critical articles and reviews.
Please send inquiries to mangiferabloom@gmail.com.

Find out more at https://www.fosteringthroughtheeyesofachild.net

1st Edition

ISBN: 978-1-7342500-3-9 (Paperback)
ISBN: 978-1-7342500-7-7 (ebook)

Library of Congress Control Number: 2020909246

Edited by Mikel Benton
Cover illustration by Michael Rohani
Book design by DesignForBooks.com

Printed in the U.S.A.

# CONTENTS

**THE EXORDIUM   IX**

Dedication   ix
How My Autobiography is Organized   xii
Conventions Used   xiv
Additional Content   xvi

**ACKNOWLEDGMENT AND OVERVIEW   XVII**

**CHAPTER 1   ONWARD BOUND TO THE UNITED STATES OF AMERICA   1**

The Awesome Touchdown   1
Home Away From Home   5
Life as a College Student   11
Okay, Let's Get to Work   14
My First Winter Wonderland   17
Frozen   20
Tropical Taste Buds   23
Warmth and Generosity   25
The Need to Adjust Academically   27
The Academic Thrust   29
Academic Transition   30
Embarking on a New Academic Frontier   34
The Passing of My Father   35
Back on Track   35
The Summer Heat   41

Job Creation Effort    41

## CHAPTER 2  GOING OUR SEPARATE WAYS    45

The Unforgettable Blizzard    48
Frozen Fruits    59
The Enormous Expenditure    59
Low-Skill to High-Tech    64
Off to the Sunny Island of Jamaica    64
The Final Stretch of My College of DuPage Academic
   Journey    66
Practical Training    69
Clash of Religion and the Cultural Norms of Society    70
Is University Possible?    75
Could I Work Just a Little Longer?    75

## CHAPTER 3  THE TREACHEROUS JOURNEY    83

Are We There Yet?    83

## CHAPTER 4  LIFE IN THE SUNSHINE STATE    95

Back to the Island to Renew My Student Visa    95
In Search of Higher Education    98
The Passing of My Mother and My Close Call with Death    101
The Boca Raton Thriller    103
Okay, Let's Get It Together    116
The Unexplainable Recovery    126
Life without a Home    127
Yet Another Reason to Celebrate    138

## CHAPTER 5  JAMAICA BOUND AFTER EIGHT YEARS OF KNOWLEDGE QUEST    141

Do I Still Have a Job with the Airports Authority of
   Jamaica?    142

## Contents

**CHAPTER 6  THE CONTINUOUS PURSUIT OF KNOWLEDGE  147**

Life as a Graduate Student  149
The MBA Journey  150

**CHAPTER 7  DO I HAVE WHAT IT TAKES TO GET A "REAL" JOB?  157**

**CHAPTER 8  THE MIRACULOUS BIRTH OF LIFE  161**

**CHAPTER 9  UNFORESEEN EVENTS  165**

Perpetual Knowledge Quest  165
Off to Adelphia Communications  167
The Bitter Pill  173
Stability for the Family  176

**CHAPTER 10  A JOB IN TIME SAVES NINE  177**

**CHAPTER 11  HER FINAL DESTINY  179**

**CHAPTER 12  LIBERTY FOR ONE  183**

**CHAPTER 13  CONVERGENCE OF THE PAST AND THE PRESENT  187**

I Think It's Time to Go to the Emergency Room  190
Could It Be My Appendix and Not Gas Pain?  191
Okay, Let's Get Back to Work  193
It's the Phone; Who Could It Be?  193
Psychological Resurgence  194

# Contents

**CHAPTER 14 THE MEMORABLE 360-JOURNEY OF MY CHILDHOOD 201**

The Sudden Loss of Loved Ones  219
Time to Turn the Page  220

**CHAPTER 15 THE JOURNEY 223**

Let's Put the Future on Hold While I Revisit the Past  224
Back to the Future  227
Intervention  232
Perception  234
The Relentless Pursuit  238
Life in All Its Glory  239

**CHAPTER 16 REUNITING WITH MY ONLY BROTHER 241**

**CHAPTER 17 HOME SWEET HOME 257**

**CHAPTER 18 THE AFFLICTED 261**

Envisioning the Unthinkable  261
Faced with a Dark Reality  263

**CONCLUSION: HOW DID I GET HERE?  267**

**UNITED STATES OF AMERICA – THE JOURNEY  273**

**APPENDIX A: THE EMOTIONAL AND PSYCHOLOGICAL EFFECT  275**

**REFERENCE  277**

# THE EXORDIUM

## Dedication

First and foremost, I would like to give God the glory for bestowing unto me health, strength, happiness, and the many other wonderful blessings of life. These undeserved gifts have provided me with life's essentials and more. They also provided me with the courage and dedication to compose my autobiography. Second, I would like to take this opportunity to pay one final tribute by dedicating this volume to the memories of three significant people. The first person is my loving and compassionate wife, Johanna Tomlinson, who has invited me into her life and has provided me with the family of a lifetime. The second person is my mother-in-law, Marlene Isaacs, who has invited me into her home and into her life and, most importantly, has been more than a mother to me. The third is my brother-in-law, Jeremi Isaacs, who has been like a brother to me since the day I came to know him.

I would like to commence by highlighting two of the more pressing questions that I keep pondering since the day I decided to share my life story. The first is, what defining message will my life experiences convey to humanity as a whole? And second, will humanity be receptive to such a message? I thought I had these questions all figured out, but

## The Exordium

the more I think about them, the more I realize that I may never be able to come up with definitive answers. However, in my quest to uncover the answers, I would hope that you join me as I traverse the final volume that constitutes my life's journey in the United States of America. At first, I thought about the possibility of conveying my story verbally. On second thought, I realized that this method would certainly not be the most effective. With that in mind, I set out to tell my story in a written form and hope to accomplish the following:

- To highlight the wonderful blessings of God that have transformed my life

- To express the overwhelming and unyielding compassion that was bestowed unto me by my foster mother, Aunt Lucy

- To establish the fact that life is not just about my inner circle or me, but also about individuals who have not been fortunate to be loved and cared for, especially throughout their early childhood and adolescent years

- To acknowledge and to credit the many individuals and institutions that have provided me with the help and support I desperately needed throughout my early childhood years

- To highlight the fact that the desire to pray and the need to persevere are the two most important characteristics that I relied on each day to overcome life's obstacles[1]

---

1 Although I have intentionally left out tangible aspects such as financial needs, it does not mean that I do not value their importance. However, the

*The Exordium*

- To demonstrate that you should never give up when you find yourself going through life's darkest moments because God is always there with you
- To shine a light on the foster care system and stress the need for us to develop and implement policies to protect children and the less fortunate
- To share my personal experiences that have allowed me to realize the undeniable parallel between my former foster parents' actions and our actions today[2]
- To provide inspiration and comfort to all, particularly the less fortunate (orphans) who have gone through or find themselves going through challenging times

Although I had the burning desire to shine a light on the many aspects of my life, including that of siblings, I found myself at a crossroads contemplating the inevitable for the following three reasons. First, I was quite fearful that I would find myself reliving the darkest and most painful memories of my past, especially those of my childhood and those concerning my only brother. Second, I wanted to live a normal life and not to be misunderstood or to be treated any differently because of my past. Third and

---

point I am conveying is this: Financial and other material possessions are not characteristics of one's being. I have highlighted this concept in detail, especially throughout the compare-and-contrast sections dealing with Aunt Lucy and my former foster parents. This have been outlined in volume 3 of my autobiography.

2 The most obvious are those perpetrated by deception, and the utter disregard for the well-being of others, especially the less fortunate. I also use this opportunity to highlight my brother's relentless cry for justice and the need to challenge hearts and minds to pursue justice and peace above ego, self-acclaimed interests, and conflicts.

final, I was too busy with school, my career, my family, and the many other priorities that have taken precedence in my life. However, after many years of being nudged continuously by an internal voice, in the year 2007, I finally decided to heed the calling and proceed with the writing of my autobiography.

Today, I am more motivated than ever because I realized that someday my daughters (Julianne, Deanna, and Anna) might have the desire to learn more about the true me but I may not be around or may not have the time to provide them with my life's story in one or two sittings. So, after thirteen long years, I have finally completed the writing of my autobiography. Today, if my daughters have any questions concerning my childhood, I am in a position to take the easy way out by just referring them to the four volumes that comprise my lengthy and, at times, interesting biography. On the one hand, I would like to see my children enjoy life to its fullest, irrespective of my childhood physical and psychological struggles. On the other hand, I hope that they do not take life for granted, thinking that the opportunities they have today were also made available to me as a child.

## How My Autobiography Is Organized

My autobiography is presented in four volumes. The first three volumes cover the unpredictable, life-changing events that occurred while I was living on the tropical island of Jamaica. The fourth reflects the transformational journey of my life after I migrated to the United States of America.

*The Exordium*

Volume 1, *The Separation* – this volume takes into account the following:

- Life with my father
- The emotional separation when my brother and I were forcefully removed from our father's care and transferred to an orphanage
- The joyous reunification when my brother and I were transferred from the orphanage back to our father's care
- The emotional separation when my brother, my sisters, and I were forcefully removed from our father's care and divvied up between orphanages
- The transfer of my brother and me from the orphanage to our mother's care
- The emotional separation when my brother and I were forcefully removed from our mother's care and returned to the orphanage

Volume 2, *Woka Man* – this volume takes into account the following:

- The transfer of my brother and me from the orphanage to a foster home
- The eternal, physical, and emotional separation that occurred between my brother and me when he was transferred to a correctional institution
- The remaining time I spent with my first foster parents, including how and why I was also removed from their care

*The Exordium*

Volume 3, *The Turning Point* – this volume takes into account the following:

- The transition to and from a temporary foster home
- When and how I was united with my wonderful, caring, loving foster mother, Aunt Lucy
- Reunion with my biological family, including my only brother
- The continuation of my academic, professional, social, and *spiritual* journey

Volume 4, *A Dream Come True* – this volume takes into account the following:

- The remaining precious and unforgettable time I spent with my wonderful, caring, loving foster mother, Aunt Lucy
- The journey to a land far, far away to fulfill my academic dream
- The unimaginable but inspiring and transformative academic, professional, social, and *spiritual* opportunities that continue to shape and reshape my life
- The miraculous birth of life and the family of a lifetime

**Conventions Used**

To maintain the originality of individual quotes, phrases, and humor, I have incorporated the Jamaican Patois (Patwa) along with the English translations. However, in

*The Exordium*

some cases, I have paraphrased both the Jamaican Patois and English translations as a way to maintain contextuality. Please bear in mind that the Jamaican Patois does not have a definitive structure. Therefore, the spelling and pronunciation of certain words could differ slightly. There are many sources and variations; however, I have relied on the *Jabari Authentic Jamaican Dictionary of the Jamic Language* as a guide (Reynolds 2006).

Although this book is my autobiography, I have taken the initiative to highlight the many acts of kindness bestowed unto me by several family members, friends, acquaintances, strangers, and prominent institutions. These individuals and institutions are the many parts that have made my life whole. They have provided me with life's essentials and more. I have also been blessed to have received a lifetime of spiritual and moral support that has guided my actions and the way I perceived my fellow humankind.

Irrespective of the many unfortunate circumstances, especially those concerning my only brother, I do hope that you will enjoy a smile and a little laughter as you read my tidbits of humor. I must also warn you that a number of my witticisms might go, swoosh, right over your head because they might be technologically funneled or skewed to a particular culture or era, or in the words of an American teenager, they might come across as lame or botched. For the humor that you do not have a clue about, you are just going to have to wave the Google magic wand for further clarification.

## Additional Content

To complement my written autobiography, I have created the www.fosteringthroughtheeyesofachild.net website to provide additional information and content, such as pictures and links for the subjects and topics that I have referred to throughout the different volumes. The reader or interested party is more than welcome to use this website to provide an ongoing discussion regarding the content of my autobiography and other topics associated with the development and well-being of children.

# ACKNOWLEDGMENT AND OVERVIEW

Johanna Tomlinson

Please bear with me while I take this opportunity to introduce and to express my sincere thanks and gratitude to several individuals, including family members and friends, whom I have mentioned throughout this volume of my autobiography.

I would like to express my sincere thanks, gratitude, and never-ending love to my wife, Johanna Tomlinson. She has opened her heart and welcomed me into her life. She has been more to me than I could ever imagine. Surely, there are just not enough words to express how much her love and her friendship mean to me. At first, it was not easy for me to understand why we were meant for each other. However, today, I can say unequivocally that she has made my life complete. Although I did not possess any material wealth, nor was I equipped to express the most romantic, elegant, and passionate words (like Cupid and Romeo), none of that mattered because she saw something in me that goes far beyond those shortcomings. She stood by me every step of the way. I can truly say that her endless love, overwhelming

## Acknowledgment and Overview

compassion, and moral support is far more than I could have ever asked of her. She has given me three wonderful daughters (Julianne, Deanna, and Anna), who constitute the greatest gift that life could ever offer. Johanna has helped me to overcome my greatest fear of becoming a husband, father, and, most important of all, a parent.

The joy of becoming a parent was manifested on November 12, 2002, with the birth of my first daughter, Julianne Tomlinson.

The bundle of joy                      Look how time flies!

The wonderful joy of life returned on February 2, 2011, with the birth of my second daughter, Deanna Tomlinson. I must admit I was still a bit nervous, but I presumed that to be nervous is normal, because each birth is unique and precious in its own way.

On July 22, 2015, the triad was formed with the precious birth of my third daughter, Anna Tomlinson. Although I thought that experiencing the birth of my third child would be something of a natural routine, once again, I must say with all clarity that every gift of life is unique and precious in its own way.

*Acknowledgment and Overview*

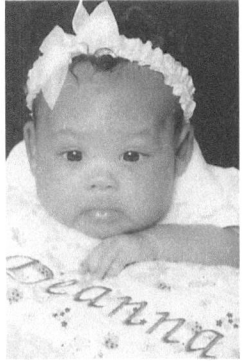  

The joy of life is wonderful and precious.

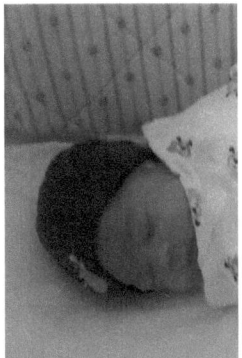  

The joy of life is wonderful and precious.

At this juncture, I would like to introduce my mother-in-law, Marlene Isaacs, and brother-in-law, Jeremi Isaacs. Marlene has been a mother to me in every way possible, while Jeremi has always been a brother and a friend. Marlene treated me with the same love and compassion that she bestowed unto her children. She opened her doors and invited me into her home and into her life. She treated me like a son, even before I had the privilege of becoming her son-in-law. At first, I was a bit skeptical because of the many horrifying in-law stories that I had heard. However,

Acknowledgment and Overview

Marlene Isaacs

Jeremi Isaacs

I came to realize that her wonderful traits are genuine and that they reflect her inner being. Also, I would like to thank her for dedicating many hours of her precious time to reading and proofreading my autobiography. The only drawback is that, by reading my autobiography, she has uncovered all my secrets. Don't worry, because after you are through reading my autobiography, you will know my secrets too. Last but certainly not the least, Jeremi has always been there when I needed someone to talk with and to discuss pressing issues or concerns. I can say, without a doubt, that I am truly blessed to have someone who has been like a brother to me.

Finally, I would like to provide you with a brief update of my only biological brother, George Tomlinson. Throughout the early stages of our childhood, Paulette, Pauline, George, and I were subjected to our father's Rastafarians doctrine. After many years of not being allowed to attend school, the Child Development Agency (CDA) took us from our father's care and placed us in different orphanages. My sisters were placed in one orphanage, while my

## Acknowledgment and Overview

brother and I were placed at another. After experiencing a roller-coaster-like, back-and-forth transition between our father, the orphanage, and our mother's care, the CDA finally transferred my brother and me to a foster home. However, instead of receiving the love and care we desperately needed, we were abused physically and psychologically by our foster parents. My brother made several unsuccessful attempts to reason with our foster parents for basic fairness and to let them (more so our foster mother) know that we deserved to be treated like human beings. In return, my brother was severely punished because of his outspokenness. He was considered to be presumptuous and ill-mannered, and, in many instances, he was accused of being an evil person and one who portrayed a sense of entitlement. He was labeled as a dog and a scavenger. Not only that, but his foster parents detested his very presence. In the end, they took him to Copse (juvenile correctional institution) without any justification other than his relentless cry for justice. My former foster parents' actions spun my brother's life into a downward spiral from which he never recovered.

This is a picture of my only brother. Today, I am distraught and heartbroken to have witnessed what had become of him. Picture Date: 2010.

## CHAPTER 1

# ONWARD BOUND TO THE UNITED STATES OF AMERICA

**The Awesome Touchdown**

On September 21, 1991, after approximately four hours of continuous cruising, the American Trans Air flight finally landed at the O'Hare International Airport in Chicago. The first thing that caught my attention was the vast difference between the Donald Sangster International Airport and O'Hare International Airport. According to my initial observation, I would conclude that O'Hare is not only many times larger than Sangster, but it appeared as though it was also larger than the entire city of Montego Bay. After this brief observation, it was time for us to disembark the aircraft. That day I had a chilling experience due to the cold wind that was blowing across the open tarmac. After disembarking the aircraft, I ran to the shuttle and shoved my way to the middle just to get away from the cold wind that was blowing through the open doors.

Before I continue with this segment, I would like to provide my fellow tropical islanders with a bit of advice.

## Chapter 1

Please do not dress in your tropical clothing when migrating to Chicago in the fall and winter seasons. Take it from me, because I am living proof of what the cold wind will do to your "tropical irie man feelings!" Anyway, after a short trip, the shuttle arrived at the main terminal. Once again, I ran from the shuttle to the main terminal to avoid the cold. Landing in Chicago for the first time presented me with a rude awakening. This was my first taste of the Windy City, but that was just a precursor because the worst was yet to come. As a matter of fact, it was only September. Therefore, we had several weeks to go before winter.

Nonetheless, the initial experience reminded me that I needed many things, including winter attire. I know you might be saying, what's up with all this cold talk, and it was only September, not January or February! Well, I do believe that I deserve a break because this was my first time leaving the tropical island of Jamaica to live in a very cold place known to everyone as the Windy City. Therefore, I deserve a pass for acting as though I had just landed at the North Pole. However, after having gone through a couple of winters, I came to realize that I had been a total chicken on the first day of my Chicago experience. I can assure you that the subzero degree sucks the "cool runnings," "no problem, man," tropical lifestyle from my body, mind, and soul. Please stay tuned because there are a lot more "chilling" episodes to come.

After clearing customs, Carolene, Prudence, Michael, and I went to the arrival area where we were greeted by Lenny, one of the senior Jamaican trainees. Just as a reminder, Lenny, Carolene, Prudence, and Michael were all past trainees of my Runaway Bay Heart Academy, who had also been awarded a two-year scholarship to study

## Onward Bound to the United States of America

hotel management in the United States of America. Lenny was now in his second year in the hotel management program. We were more than fortunate because not only did the college provide us with transportation service from the airport, but we were given the royal limousine treatment as well. I remember the limousine driver came out, opened the door, and, after we were all seated, closed the door, then took our luggage and loaded it into the trunk. This was my first limousine ride, and I was definitely feeling like a high-profile celebrity.

On the way from the airport, I kept looking out the windows, observing the landscape, the magnificent buildings, the highways, and the hundreds of motor vehicles that were swooshing by. Actually, I was feasting my eyes on just about any and everything that was within my peripheral vision. The highways are superior when compared to the Jamaican roads. The impressive highways and the vast number of vehicles gave me the impression that everyone appeared to be in a mad rush. For sure it was not the "soon come," laid-back Jamaican culture I was accustomed to. Instead, it was welcome to the "warp speed," "beam me up," American way of life.

After the long and scenic ride, we finally arrived in the city of Glen Ellyn. The limousine driver navigated around the Rambletree apartment complex and finally stopped at the entrance to one of the large apartment buildings. As soon as the driver opened the door and I stepped out of the car, it appeared as though I had been at this very place before. I did not give it much thought because I was very tired from the previous days' rigorous activities. With that said, I picked up my bags and followed Lenny into the apartment. The leasing office was closed for the day, so we

## Chapter 1

were unable to finalize the rental process. With that said, Prudence, Carolene, Michael, and I ended up spending the night with the senior batch of Jamaican students.

That night I had a difficult time sleeping due to the overwhelming mixed emotions that were plaguing my mind. I must admit that it was not just my financial situation that I was worried about, but I was also questioning my ability to complete the hotel management training program successfully. Nonetheless, I did manage to get a couple of hours of sleep, most likely after remembering the comforting words of my foster mother.

Sunday, September 22, 1991, after spending my first night in the United States of America, I woke up to the dawn of a new day. There I was, thinking how this day signified the beginning of a new chapter that was about to transform my life in a significant way. Okay, I should not be projecting too far into the future because there were many pressing issues to accomplish first. After breakfast, one of the senior Jamaican trainees took us to the rental complex so that we could complete the necessary paperwork for our apartment. The living arrangement was made affordable because the senior trainees had discovered that it was more economical for us to incorporate a dormitory-style living accommodation rather than each person having his or her own apartment. I was quite familiar with this living arrangement while living at the Garland Hall orphanage, my former foster parents', and the Runaway Bay HEART Academy. Therefore, sharing an apartment with three other people was a welcoming choice for me. Besides, it was more economical for us to divide the expenses among four people.

With that in mind, we executed the "divide and conquer" economic model and rented a two-bedroom apartment. To offset some of the initial costs, the college made the security deposit on the apartment and arranged for the leasing of the furniture. Faculty members also donated pots, pans, and other kitchen utensils. As for food, Carlos and Rick, two of the cafeteria workers, provided us with regular leftover meals from the cafeteria. However, this wonderful opportunity did not last for long because, shortly after that, the college outsourced the operation of the cafeteria to other food vendors. Well, there is no complaint on my part because I did enjoy some tasty leftovers.

**Home Away From Home**

Back to my first day's events. After all the paperwork was finally completed, we moved into our apartment at Cedar Lane, Glen Ellyn, Illinois. The apartment was quite small for four people, but it was not a problem for me because, over the years, I had learned to adapt to the environment in which I found myself. Moreover, my objective was to take full advantage of this once-in-a-lifetime opportunity. However, as I stepped into the apartment and looked out the window, I noticed that everything looked quite familiar. It was as though I had been at that very same location looking out the window at the brick buildings that surrounded the apartment. As I continued to look out the window, "Slowly but surely," in the words of Celine Dion, "it's all coming back to me now." It was the unfolding of a dream I had some seven years earlier.

For me to put everything into context, I will have to take you back seven years down memory lane. This

## Chapter 1

dream occurred in the year 1984, while I was living with my loving and caring foster mother, Fredricka Lucy Brady (Aunt Lucy). In this dream, I found myself in a strange place, surrounded by several large, reddish, iron-colored buildings. Although the outsides of the buildings were badly in need of a paint job, I was amazed by how beautiful the insides were. It was not just the buildings that caused me to reflect on this dream, but also the fact that I found myself in a school-like setting surrounded by a vast number of Caucasian students. The context of this dream led me to conclude that it was not a typical Jamaican school setting. In addition to the buildings and the classroom-like setting, I also saw several mango trees that were all laden with blossom and young fruits. Although I remembered every detail of this dream, I did not have a clue what it really meant. I usually do have dreams, but most of them were haunting nightmares due to the psychological effects of my childhood. Therefore, I would not put much thought into trying to understand what they really meant. Besides, I tend to forget most of my dreams by the time I am awake. However, this dream kept buzzing around in my mind. It was as clear as crystal, and I remember it in its entirety. Despite having this dream buzzing around in my mind, I decided not to talk about it.

However, all that changed one day when I found myself discussing this very dream with one of the church elders, James Smith. I told him that I had a dream in which I found myself in a strange place, surrounded by several large buildings. The outsides of the buildings were really ugly and strange-looking, but the insides were beautiful and quite comfortable. I went on to let him know that I also found myself sitting in a classroom-like setting with predominantly white students. Finally, I told him that I saw several mango trees laden with young fruits. Immediately, he interrupted me and said, "What else did you see on the mango trees?" I told him that in addition to the young fruits, the mango trees were also laden with blossoms.

With no hesitation whatsoever, he interpreted my dream by saying, "Your entire dream is about you going to school in the United States of America." My first reaction was to infer that he was only saying so because I had told him about the classroom-like setting and the Caucasian students. However, he did not stop there. He went on to let me know that the young fruits signified hardship in the beginning, but that I should not worry because the blossoms signified prosperity that would follow. I told him that I did not understand his interpretation, because one would think that a tree laden with young fruits signified prosperity. Not only that, but his precept came across as illogical because the bloom comes before the fruit, so one would think that the prosperity would come first followed by hardship.

However, he reinforced his point by saying that the young fruits were a sign of hardship in the initial stage, but the blossoms represent prosperity after that. His interpretation sounded like "the chicken and the egg" philosophy, so I decided that it was not worth the effort to extend the conversation. Anyway, after his interpretation of the mango trees, I decided not to seek his interpretation regarding the ugly buildings because they might represent a "not so pleasant" outcome for me. That was the last time I had any conversation regarding this dream except when I told my Child Development Agency officer that I would be going to school in the United States, which she thought

## Chapter 1

was noteworthy and logged it in my file. I discovered this to be the case some twenty-five years later.

Although I believe that with God all things are possible, at the time, I was not fully convinced by Mr. Smith's interpretation of my dream. Here is the reason for my doubt. I saw myself as an orphan child who was not expecting anything more than the very basics, such as food, clothes, and shelter. This was the case because my foster mother resided in a district that would be considered at or below the poverty level when compared to developed nations. She could barely afford the basic necessities, so I would never be so ambitious as to entertain a conversation about attending college in Jamaica, much less in the United States of America. The odds were stacked against me so high, I just could not see how this would ever be possible. Even if I had the financial means and the necessary contacts, I would have to be an outstanding scholar from a prestigious institution to be awarded a scholarship to study in the United States. However, as you can see, I was using current and former constraints to restrict future progress concerning what is possible with God.

This dream reappeared at that very moment when I found myself in the United States of America, standing at the very window, observing the very surroundings, just as it had been revealed unto me seven years earlier. I looked around for the mango trees but did not see any, not even the trees with the young fruits. However, I did not need to see the mango trees to be entirely convinced that I was truly in the United States of America to further my academic career. As the saying goes, "Seeing is believing." So not seeing any of the young mangoes meant that it should be all "cool runnings" from this point forward. Well, later you and I will be the judge of this premise.

Back to the moment at hand. After spending some time in my splendid apartment, I went back to the senior Jamaicans' apartment, where I enjoyed a typical Jamaican Sunday dinner and relaxed for the afternoon. I also learned that no matter where a Jamaican migrates to, he or she refuses to give up on the Jamaican Sunday tradition. After dinner, the senior Jamaicans gave us a tour of the college. I was amazed by the grand size (*más grande*) of the college. Its magnitude was beyond my wildest imagination. When compared to the Montego Bay community college, this college was many, many times larger. In fact, the Montego Bay Community College could literally play hide-and-seek inside the DuPage campus. That day, we toured the computer lab, the library, the gymnasium, and the other accessible areas. It was undoubtedly a remarkable sight.

After we were through with the tour, we went grocery shopping because we had absolutely no food in the apartment.Once again, we relied on Lenny to give us a ride because we had no means of transportation. Besides, we were not yet familiar with our surroundings. The minute I arrived and went inside the supermarket (Jewel-Osco), I just could not come to terms with what I was seeing. It was hard to imagine that I was in one grocery store. I had never seen a supermarket of such size before, especially when compared with the ones I was accustomed to in Jamaica. I just could not understand why most of the buildings in the United States had to be so huge! They were like superstructures. I guess living on an island with less than three million people makes it hard to fathom a country with over one hundred times that many people.

The other first impression that I could not come to terms with was the pricing structure. It seemed as though everything was dirt cheap. Back in Jamaica, I was accustomed to things costing ten times more (relatively speaking). So there I was, shopping away as if everything came cheaper by the dozen. I certainly was not thinking about the relative cost structure. Neither did I have sufficient cash on hand for all the things that I stuffed into the shopping cart. Lenny was quite astonished when he returned and saw us with a giant shopping cart filled with groceries. He intervened before we made our way to the checkout and said, "Laud Jeezas, a weh unnu guh pickup summuch sinting fa?" ("Lord Jesus, why did you guys pick up so many things?") Lenny had dropped us off at Jewel so that we could pick up the essentials, not to go on a grand shopping spree. I guess we were only concerned about how much cheaper things appeared to have been when compared to Jamaica. However, that day, I had my first rude awakening because I had to return most of the items to the shelves.

I also found out that I was grossly mistaken, because I had not yet grasped the relative economic factor. That is, regarding a "dollar for a dollar," things were not cheap when compared to the minimum hourly wage. With that said, I quickly learned how to economize based on my first shopping experience. From that point forward, I adopted a more economical model by doing all my grocery shopping at Aldi. Concerning quality, service, and ambiance, Aldi was no comparison to Jewel. However, for individuals like me who were strapped for cash, Aldi was considered a lifesaver. The produce and other necessities were much more affordable when compared to the upscale supermarkets. There goes a little food for your thought.

After my first day's expenses, which included the apartment, grocery shopping, and other school-related costs, it appeared as though I had run into the "inelasticity of demand" economic model. Thanks to my USA college knowledge, all these sophisticated business terminologies keep rolling off my tongue. Anyway, after that dramatic grocery shopping experience, we decided to end all shopping and head on home.

That night we sat around and talked for a while. We spent most of our free time talking because we did not have a television in the apartment. However, that routine changed when we received a small black and white television. That night, after we had nothing else to talk about, we went to bed because the following day was the beginning of our two-year college program. Seeing that it was my second night, and I had already overcome much of the anxiety, I was able to get a good night's sleep. Even so, it seemed that the minute I dozed off, "It's morning again in America." Hmmm, where have I heard this phrase before? Oh! It was coined by Ronald Reagan (the Big Gipper).

**Life as a College Student**

It was now Monday morning, September 23, 1991, a day that has registered in my memory to this very day. That morning when I woke up, I was well-rested and very much rejuvenated. I showered, got dressed, and ate a bologna sandwich for breakfast. By the way, this was my first time eating bologna. My roommate volunteered to make breakfast and, boy oh boy, did she fry the bologna to a crisp.

## Chapter 1

Based on what I know now, she should have taken the bologna out of the pack, placed it on the bread, and, *voilà!* breakfast is served. For a reason unknown to me, Jamaicans tend to recook all pre-cooked meats. Anyway, after eating the crispy bologna sandwich, we set out on foot to the college. The temperature felt much colder than the previous two days, but bearable. The apartment was located approximately a mile from the college, which was to our advantage because our feet were the only means of transportation we had.

I was amazed by the vast number of students and vehicles that filled the parking lots. The parking lots that had been partially empty the previous day were now completely packed with vehicles. After navigating our way through the crowded parking lots, we finally made it into the building. I was once again amazed by the vast number of students who were roaming every square inch of the building. It was like fighting my way through a crowded marketplace. Upon arrival, we were introduced to Richard Wood, executive dean of instructional and international education. After we were through with the welcoming session, it was time to meet the faculty and staff members of the hospitality (hotel management) program. First, we were introduced to George Macht, the coordinator of the hospitality program. Then we were introduced to Ms. Cathy and Mr. Thielman, the full-time instructors, who also assisted with the coordination of the hospitality program. Mr. Wood and Mr. Macht were the architects of the student exchange program.

Mr. Macht went over the program requirements and then assisted us with the selection of our courses for the first college term. He registered us FOODS 101, HOTEL

100, and FOODS 202. Mr. Macht taught the Introduction to Hotel Management (HOTEL 100) course and collaborated with Mr. Thielman on the Introduction to Food Preparation (FOODS 101) course. Mr. Kezinski taught the Merchandising (FOODS 202) course.

It was time for my first session, Introduction to Hotel Management, taught by Mr. Macht. As soon as I stepped into the classroom, it was like déjà vu. The dream I had seven years earlier was once again being played back like a movie right before my eyes. That is, this was the identical classroom setting that I had witnessed in my dream; the one in which I was sitting amongst many Caucasian students. By this time, the mango trees that were laden with blossoms and young fruits were the only aspect of my dream that had not yet been revealed in a literal form. To be frank, I would have welcomed the mango blooms, but under no circumstances was I looking forward to seeing those young mangoes of my dream.

Although the students were very open and friendly, I did not participate in any of the class discussions because I was afraid that my Jamaican accent and limited grasp of English grammar would get in the way. Not only that, but I could still hear my former foster mother's humiliating remarks echoing in my ears because I was unable to speak fluently. This fear manifested itself many times, most notably through the initial stage of my college career. However, despite my fear of public speaking, I found the class to be very informative and could not wait to do it all over again the next day.

The first day's class sessions were dedicated to getting us acquainted with the program requirements. However as the days progress, we spent an average of two hours in

## Chapter 1

each class session, and anywhere from two to three hours for the Food Preparation labs. The Food Preparation labs provided us with the opportunity to prepare all sorts of dishes and to eat them too. Please stick around for the drama that my Jamaican roommate and I unleashed in the kitchen when we decided to "Jamaicanize" our cooking.

Immediately after my morning class, we were taken to the Social Security Administration office so that we could obtain our social security cards. Getting our social security cards was a top priority because we had to work twenty hours per week with the college so that we could use the proceeds to cover expenses such as food, school supplies, and room and board. Once we had obtained our social security cards, it was time to seek on-campus employment.

Later that afternoon, a faculty member from the hospitality program inquired of me regarding my prior work experience. I told her that I had worked at the Donald Sangster International Airport in Jamaica for the past three years as an electrician and would have no problem working in such capacity. I also filled out a job interest form to reflect the above experience. To be clear, has anyone heard me say anything about assuming a janitorial role? No sir! I certainly did not!

**Okay, Let's Get to Work**

After all the necessary work requirements were in place, one of the faculty members took me to a work area and told me to have a seat and that someone would be with me shortly. While I was there sitting in the room, thinking about my first electrical engineering job in the United States of America, my overambitious thoughts were interrupted by a gentleman who came up to me and asked, "Are you the person who applied for the student aid work?"

I replied with an enthusiastic, "Yes, I am!"

Then he said, "Hi, my name is Cliff, and I will be your supervisor."

To which I replied, "Nice to meet you, Cliff."

Finally, he said, "Wait here; I will be right back." To my surprise, he returned with a janitorial cart that was filled with all sorts of cleaning apparatus and accessories. It was equipped with the following items: a great big bucket, a giant wet mop, a humongous swivel sweeper, and a dust rag that was wrapped around a flat metal object resembling a masonry finishing trowel. In addition to the above items, it had a small hand sweeper and dustpan set, a spray bottle that was filled with vinegar (which at first I thought was water) and, last but not least, several boxes of chalk, dry markers, and erasers. At first, I was a bit confused, wondering why an electrician like me was being presented with all these cleaning devices. My second reaction was, where are my electrical tools? Okay, you can go ahead laugh, because you probably have figured out that "I ain't gonna" (US Patois: "I am not going to") be working as an electrician. Instead of receiving a position in the electrical engineering department, I was now the new College of DuPage Jamaican janitor.

Nonetheless, it was no time to be fastidious or to indulge in non-valuable pride. Instead, it was time to roll up my sleeves and focus on the prize ahead. Surely, I was not going to let anything, and I mean anything, get in the way of this wonderful opportunity. No sir! I was not going to let non-valuable pride and ego deny me of this opportunity!

## Chapter 1

With that said, I accepted my new janitorial assignment with pride. Although I worked for the college, I reported directly to ServiceMaster. ServiceMaster was responsible for all the janitorial aspects of the college. I spent the next two years performing all sorts of janitorial duties, which included cleaning classrooms, bathrooms, athletes' locker rooms, and windows; transporting furniture; setting up and breaking down furniture for different functions across the campus; and just about any other "man-u-labor" tasks that needed to be done.

My first assignment was to clean and restock supplies for all the classrooms located on the second floor. The actual job functions included sweeping and spot mopping the floor, rearranging the chairs and desks, cleaning the blackboards and whiteboards, and replacing the dry erasers, markers, and chalk. Occasionally, I would remove the trash from the classrooms. This was mostly my job function throughout the weekdays. However, on the weekends, it was a lot more intense, which I will discuss shortly.

Here is a preview of my "warp speed" college life in the United States of America. It was normal for me to leave home anywhere around 7:30 a.m. and return around 10:00 p.m. First I would attend my classes; then I would work for four hours in the afternoon; then I would go to the library and study for three to four hours; finally I would go back home and continue studying for another four to five hours. Academic life in the United States was quite a drastic transformation from the Jamaican laidback (soon come man) academic lifestyle I had been accustomed to. I can assure you that the fast-paced academic structure posed a significant challenge for me in the initial stage, mostly due to my slow-paced learning. I stress academic life because life was very hectic for my brother and me, especially throughout the time we were living with our former foster parents (details are documented in volume 2 of my autobiography).

On the weekends, my job function would include tasks that were more heavy-duty in nature. These included cleaning windows, buffing or stripping and re-waxing floors, and cleaning and restocking restrooms with supplies. However, the most difficult of the weekend tasks was the cleaning of the athletes' locker rooms. Here is why this was the most daunting of all the tasks. Whenever it rained, cleaning the locker rooms after a football game required extensive janitorial work. The mess factor and odor level were at their highest order. For us to tackle this job, my coworkers and I would use all the available equipment that was at our disposal. There were tape scraps, tape balls, bandages, mud, grass, and a lot more mud all over the place. And don't even mention the clogged toilets and the many pieces of sweaty sportswear that were left behind. Sometimes I wonder if it were migration season and a herd of wildebeest had just passed through the building. Also, whenever it snowed, the mixture of salt and snow would leave behind a residue that would take quite a bit of elbow grease to remove. Nevertheless, it was a job to do, and someone had to do the job.

**My First Winter Wonderland**

I remember the first day it snowed! Yes, I remember it as if it was just yesterday. My roommates and I were at home when, all of a sudden, we looked out the apartment window and, lo and behold, we saw this white, flaky stuff falling from the sky.

## Chapter 1

It was so amazing! We simply could not contain ourselves. We ran outside and started catching the snowflakes. Finally I had the opportunity to experience this exciting phenomenon that I used to see broadcast on the television and heard about while living in Jamaica. After approximately fifteen minutes, we had enough and went back inside. We were not dressed for that kind of weather. The light Jamaican clothing we wore was simply no match for the Chicago cold. That night it snowed lightly but not enough to cause a visible accumulation. This exciting phenomenon happened several times, but I was always amazed by it. This weather condition is what people living in Chicago call snow flurries.

One day, or should I say one night, it started snowing quite heavily. It was a beautiful sight to see the clusters of snowflakes pouring down from the night sky. The following morning, I was awakened by a rather strange noise that sounded like a large metal object being dragged all over the pavement. It went on for a good while. I was unable to sleep, so I got up and looked out the window, and there it was, the snowplow. It was hard at work, clearing the streets. My first reaction was to drink a hot cup of chocolate and go right back to bed. Well, that was only wishful thinking because I had a long college day ahead of me. And seeing all that snow outside, I realized that I needed a winter jacket. With no other option, I had to wear an old, worn-out winter jacket that had been given to me by one of the senior Jamaicans. As soon as I ventured outside, all I could see were piles and piles of snow on both sides of the streets and sidewalks. The cars in the parking lots were partially covered with snow. Surely winter had arrived. It was like witnessing something from a winter wonderland movie.

I just could not believe that I was experiencing my first snowy day. I did not have a car, so the only way to get to and from school was on foot. To my surprise, all of my available shortcuts were blocked with snow. I decided to "plow" my way through the piled-up snow instead of using the longer route along the roadway. In some areas, I found myself covered in snow all the way up to my knees. Despite the snow, the parking lots were packed with vehicles. It seemed as though nothing, not even a heavy downpour of snow, was able to stop or slow down the day's progress.

After struggling through the snow and the crowded parking lots, I finally made it to school. It was a blessing to be on the inside, where it was warm and cozy. I hurried to the restroom and dislodged the snow that was melting away in my shoes. I also realized that I needed a pair of snow boots, which I bought shortly after that.

Plowing my way through the piled-up snow was just the beginning of my first real winter drama. Each day the temperature would drop, and it would get a lot colder than the previous day. This lifestyle and environmental condition was certainly not the Jamaican life that I was accustomed to. I started to suffer from nosebleeds, chapped lips, and other dry and itchy skin conditions. In fact, that day while I was sitting in class, I felt as though an entire legion of ants were attacking me from all sides. I felt my entire body itching. I literally could not rest my back against the chair due to the severe discomfort I was experiencing. Whenever I moved, it felt as though my skin were being torn apart. Not knowing what was really causing my discomfort, I started wondering if there were some sort of bed bug roaming the apartment.

## Chapter 1

As soon as I was through with my morning classes, I ran home so that I could determine what was subjecting me to such discomfort. When I reached home and removed my clothes, I could not believe my own eyes! My skin was dried to the point that I could literally see cracks and scales. I mean, it was white and flaky looking. That was when I realized that I needed a gallon of lotion to soothe my dry and itchy skin. I did not have any lotion because, all this time, I had thought that lotion was only for women. Prior to this day, my Jamaican attitude was that real men do not need lotion! Well, I had to put my Jamaican male pride aside, sneak into the girls' room, and apply some of their soothing lotion to my body. "Oh! What a relief it was!" From that point forward, I made a concerted effort to stock up on many bottles of the affordable Vaseline® Intensive Lotion. I also found that I needed a couple of chapsticks to soothe my chapped lips as well.

**Frozen**

After I was through with my classes, I went to work as I usually did. To my surprise, or more like to my dismay, my supervisor told me that he had a new assignment for me. He went into the storage room and, within a couple of minutes, returned with a huge shovel and what appeared to be a fertilizer spreader filled with salt. He presented me with both items and told me that my job was to remove the snow from the access points and sidewalks throughout the campus and then apply the coarse salt to the said areas. I wanted to protest this task because I thought this was certainly not a thoughtful job assignment for a Jamaican. However, before you label me a chicken, I want you to

## Onward Bound to the United States of America

take a deep breath and think about what had just happened. First, can you imagine a Jamaican who has lived his entire life in Jamaica (twenty-three years, to be precise), who suddenly finds himself living in Chicago, and his first winter assignment is to shovel snow! What next! Are they going to ask him to join the Jamaican bobsled team too? And just don't stop there, what about ice skating, hockey, skiing? Or, what the heck, let's go ice fishing while we are at it! Now that you have put this strange phenomenon into perspective, let me go ahead and fill you in on my first winter assignment.

I am not sure what my supervisor had on his mind when he assigned me this task. Probably he did it just to enjoy a good laugh, because he knew quite well that I had just migrated from Jamaica and had never experienced this type of winter before. Anyway, let's give him the benefit of the doubt because he simply was not thinking. Once again, I did not want to complain because getting my education was my top priority. Therefore, this job assignment was worth the sacrifice, especially when compared to the wonderful academic opportunity that was made available to me. Despite the cold, I thought it would be a fun job as well. So there I was, bracing the cold while shoveling snow and applying salt to the access points and sidewalks across the campus.

However, after being out in the cold for over three hours, I started experiencing a weird unexplainable feeling. My whole body started twitching, followed by an achy feeling. I felt as though I had been through a rigorous and complete workout. With that many aches and pains radiating throughout my body, I decided that I had enough, so I went inside and sat in the break room. I simply did not have the energy to finish that brutal task. I remember sitting in the break room until it was time for me to clock out. After leaving work, I usually went to the library and studied for several hours. However, the way I was feeling that afternoon, I went straight home. The only thing I remember was that I opened the door to the apartment, went into my room, and finally lay face down on the bed.

When my roommates came home later that evening, they were unable to get inside the apartment because I had locked the door with the deadbolt, which is forbidden during the day. Actually, we should only have used the deadbolt at night when everyone was inside the apartment. With that said, they tried to get in but could not. They resorted to banging away on the door, but I simply did not hear them because I was out cold. Having no other choice, they decided to go to the college library and study for a while. After they returned, somewhere around 10:00 p.m., they still had to bang on the door and yell my name several times before I finally heard them. I jumped out of my sleep, coma, unconsciousness, or whatever I was in, and opened the door. Based on what my roommates told me, I would conclude that I had experienced a mild case of hypothermia because I had not been properly dressed for extended exposure to the cold.

This near-death experience taught me the valuable lesson that having proper winter attire was critical for my survival. I also learned rather quickly that the clothes I had brought with me from Jamaica were no match for the brutal Chicago winter. And the old worn-out jacket I had was certainly not keeping me warm but, instead, was giving me what I would describe as a "shocking experience." Why was this jacket causing me to be zapped whenever I came into contact with any metal object? The shocking experience was caused by the exposed wool that would generate static electricity when rubbed against my other clothing. This would give me a good zap whenever I came in contact with any metal object or even another person through a simple handshake. It was so bad that I had developed a genuine fear whenever I had to open or close a door or even shake hands with someone. Therefore, I seldom used the worn-out jacket. Now, I needed a good winter jacket and other winter attire. Unfortunately, I did not have the disposable income to meet this important need. Once again, I was rescued by another person who was a true reflection of the good Samaritan (Biblical reference). This person provided me with several years' worth of warm clothing.

**Tropical Taste Buds**

Before I start chirping about the person who was responsible for this good deed, I would like to fill you in on two dramatic cooking episodes that made it possible for me to cross paths with this kind and generous person. These dramatic episodes started when the instructor, Mr. Rasmussen, allowed Michael and me to collaborate on the first set of food preparation labs. However, he had to separate us because he found out rather quickly that allowing two Jamaicans to collaborate on food preparation that involved classical dishes was certainly not a good idea. The reason was that Michael and I would deviate from the actual recipe and instructions concerning the cooking time and the recommended amount of spices. We strongly believed that there was only one way to prepare meat, and that was spicy and overdone. Our philosophy was, regardless of

## Chapter 1

what the instructions stipulated, "Let's spice it up and cook it some more."

Okay, let's get cooking. Our first Food Prep lab was to prepare sautéed beef. We followed the recipe as recommended, but the outcome did not light up our Jamaican taste buds. With that said, we continued to add spicy ingredients, while extending the cooking time. After we were through, the instructor conducted a taste test. Boy, oh boy! Mr. Rasmussen made a big mistake when he took a couple of pieces of our sautéed beef and stuffed them into his mouth. By the expression on his face, I could see that it was way too spicy for him. Immediately, he rushed to the faucet, filled a tall glass with water, and gulped it down quickly. After he was through, he yelled out with a stern voice, "Whose dish is this?" Michael and I quietly acknowledged that it was ours, and that was when he laid down his judgment upon us. He said, "You two Mexicans, this is not the way we cook in America. This dish is way too spicy! Did you not follow the instructions?" All of the students had a good laugh because the spice must have gotten to his brain for him to think that Jamaicans were Mexicans.

One would think that Michael and I had learned our lesson but, in fact, we had not. A couple of days later, we charcoaled and overspiced an expensive piece of steak. In Jamaica, we are used to cooking our beef until it is nice and dark, with zero pink-like appearance and substance. So, having the island-style cooking ingrained in our minds and digital sensory, we spiced and burned every ounce of protein out of the steak. I still remember that very moment when Mr. Rasmussen sliced off three pieces of the steak and noticed that it was well done all the way through. Once again, he shouted in a concerned manner, "Whose steak is this?" Michael and I owned up quickly, because we thought that we were about to receive well-deserved accolades. However, instead of showering us with praise, he reprimanded us, saying, "Listen! I don't know what you do with your steak in Jamaica, but in America we do not eat charcoal!"

Mr. Rasmussen was quite a comedian too. He had every right to be upset because this was not the first or the second time that Michael and I had deviated from the recipe and cooking instructions. In retrospect, I believe that we were more concerned with preparing the meals so that we could have something to eat afterward, rather than following the actual instructions. Anyway, from that point forward, Mr. Rasmussen decided that Michael and I should no longer collaborate on any of the food preparation labs. Separating us was for our own good, because we probably would have ended up failing the practical portion of the Food Preparation course if we had been allowed to continue "Jamaicanizing" the meals.

**Warmth and Generosity**

For our next very important lab project, Mr. Rasmussen told me to team up with Lorie/Laurie. I am not quite sure about the spelling of her name, but I will stick with Lorie until proven otherwise. With that said, I decided to reach out to my new lab partner through a couple of icebreaker conversations. During one of our conversations, she said, "So, you are from Jamaica?"

My first reaction was, I guess she was not in class when we had the cooking dramas, because everyone present was well aware that Michael and I were Jamaicans, not Mexicans. Anyway, I said, "Yes."

## Chapter 1

"Cool," she replied, then asked, "So, how long have you been living in Chicago?"

To which I replied, "Since September," referring to September 1991.

One conversation led to the next, and she asked, "Have you gone shopping for your winter clothes yet?" Instead of replying with a resounding, "No, I have not!" I showed her the jacket I had with me. Then she said, "That is not going to keep you warm! You will freeze to death wearing that thing!"

I followed up by asking, "How cold does it get?"

She replied, "The actual temperature can drop below zero, and the wind chill is what gets you." I had no idea of subzero temperature, much less understood the concept of wind chill. Not to make a short story longer, she concluded by saying, "Don't worry, I am going to get you some warm clothes because we have quite a few that nobody is wearing."

Our conversation ended there because we had to get cooking. Now that I was under the strict supervision of Lorie, there was no way she would allow me to transform the chicken à la king and the chicken fricassee into "chicken à la jerk" and "chicken jerkassee." After we were through preparing the dishes, Mr. Rasmussen came over and conducted a taste test. This time, he did not have a reason to rush to the faucet for a glass of water, as he had when Michael and I were lab partners. After class, Lorie said goodbye and reminded me that she would bring the warm clothes to our next class session.

The following class session, Lorie presented me with a large bag that was filled with a wide variety of jackets and other winter attire. Without this generous gift, it would have cost me quite a fortune if I had to purchase the assortment of warm clothing that she had provided me. The winter attire kept me warm throughout five Chicago winters. Once again, I would like to stress the point that kind deeds such as this should always be recognized and be remembered. Therefore, I would like to take this opportunity to say a big thank you to Lorie for her genuine act of kindness.

**The Need to Adjust Academically**

As the school term progressed, I was very concerned with the pace at which the professors were teaching the courses. What I had failed to realize was the fact that the school system in the United States was far different from what I had been accustomed to in Jamaica. Throughout my academic years in Jamaica, I had been accustomed to using just one textbook per subject for the entire school year. That is, I would use one math textbook for the entire year, not a different one every quarter or semester. On the one hand, the Jamaican approach to learning had one big advantage; that is, it provided the slow-learner students like me with enough time to understand the material. On the other hand, when compared to the United States or other more developed nations, the Jamaican academic approach took the individual significantly longer time to complete the same volume of work. However, as it pertains to learning, I should not be complaining about the United States' fast-pace academic system because I was always in need of a lot more time just to keep up with my peers.

With that said, my first order of business was to go back to my all-night study sessions. However, I found out rather

Chapter 1

quickly that the DuPage college was not like the Runaway Bay HEART Academy, where I could just lock myself in a classroom and study all night. Let me explain my rationale with a real-life encounter. There I was at the college, sitting in one of the classrooms studying away as if time were at a standstill. Just before closing, one of the security guards came by and told me to wrap up my study because the campus would be closing shortly. Instead of heeding his command, I turned off the lights and sat in the dark, hoping that he would not notice that I was in the classroom when he returned. Guess what, my wish came true. The security guard came by, locked the classroom door, and did not notice that I was sitting quietly in the dark. After he was through locking all the classroom doors, I turned on the lights and continued with my studies. While I was there studying with no regard for the college-designated study hours, a rather large, terminator-looking security guard opened the door and, crudely asked, "What are you doing?"

To which I replied, "Studying, sir."

He followed up by saying, "No, you're not! That was two hours ago! You are now trespassing!" The minute I heard the word trespassing, my knees started shaking. I thought I was about to be arrested. Luckily for me, that did not happen. I was relieved when he told me that I needed to get my things together and leave the premises immediately. With no hesitation whatsoever, I gathered my things and vacated the college. In the words of Jamaican DJ, Beenie Man, "Mi haffi flee." From that point forward, I learned a valuable lesson that the College of DuPage campus is no place for an all-nighter like me.

To adjust to the United States' fast-paced academic system, I spent most of my time (night and day) studying.

I had to learn speed-reading techniques, while at the same time trying to retain the information in my short-term memory. As soon as I was through with one exam, I had to flush my memory just to make way for another. The fast-paced learning was not my only challenge. My other challenge was with the approach or technique that I was using with regard to the multiple-choice exams. In Jamaica, I had been accustomed to the essay testing method, which allowed free-form answers. That is, if I did not know the specific answer to a question, then I would write all I knew about the subject, hoping to gain a point or two from the teacher. Initially, I did not do well on the multiple-choice exams because I would tend to overanalyze each question, and before I knew it, I was out of time. There were times when I would second-guess myself and change my answer, only to find out that my first choice had been the correct one. So here is my take on this scenario. The more time that I spent going over a particular test question, the greater the probability that I would end up choosing the wrong answer. One of my instructors would remind me on several occasions that my first choice was most likely the correct choice. However, as I continued to sit multiple-choice exams, I learned the art of narrowing down the choices to two possible answers.

**The Academic Thrust**

Although I was a bit nervous at first, my core conviction kept reminding me that with hard work and relentless perseverance, I could make it through the program. At the end of the first term, I was successful in all my courses. I was literally jumping for joy. It was a wonderful feeling to know that I had overcome one of my worst fears of not being able to succeed at the college level in the United States of America. I also made the president's list. Even to this day, I am still trying to figure out the benefits that are associated with this president's list. Regardless of the benefit, I was happy for any and every morale boost I could get. It's a pleasure for me to present you with a copy of my report card for my first college term in the United States of America.

```
                              1991 FALL  QUARTER
COURSE      DESCRIPTION     IAI CR HRS  HRS ATT  GR  HRS ERN  HON PTS   GPA
FOODS 101   QUANTITY PREP I      5:00    5:00    A    5:00    20:00
HOTEL 100   INTRO HOSP INDUS     5:00    5:00    B    5:00    15:00
FOODS 202   MERCHANDISING        3:00    3:00    A    3:00    12:00
       QUARTER TOTALS           13:00   13:00         13:00   47:00    3:61
    CUMULATIVE TOTALS           13:00   13:00         13:00   47:00    3:61
PRESIDENTS LIST
```

## Academic Transition

One day while I was getting ready to register for my second college term, I remember browsing through the college catalog and, lo and behold, I discovered that, in addition to the hospitality field, the college also offered degrees in other areas, which included the digital and microprocessor technology (DMT) program. This program really caught my attention. My curiosity regarding this DMT major was heightened even more when I happened to notice several students in a particular classroom building electronic circuits. I was determined to speak with the instructor, so I sat outside the classroom and waited for the class to go on break.

As soon as the class went on break, I went inside and told the professor, Mr. Wuollet, that learning about electronics and computers had always been my dream. After listening to me patiently, Mr. Wuollet replied in a soft tone of voice, saying, "I do not have enough time to explain what the program is all about right now but, I tell you what, you are more than welcome to come back later and I will provide you with more information about the program." I asked him what time, and he replied, "Somewhere around 9:30 p.m." With that said, I hurried back to the janitorial department, put away my cleaning apparatus, hurried back upstairs, and sat outside the DMT classroom, salivating like Pavlov's dog.

Before I proceed, I would like to fill you in on a little knowledge crave I developed while attending the College of DuPage. The DMT program was not the only program that I was fascinated or thrilled about. Most important were the science, technology, engineering, and math classes. On many occasions, while I was removing the trash from the classrooms, I would stand by the pane of glass that is adjacent to the door and watch as the professor taught the class. I remember the professor would open the door and ask, "May I help you?" I would reply by saying that I was there to remove the trash. Who was I kidding? I was not there just to remove the trash! No sir! I was there for the knowledge. Okay, it is evident that I was a bit biased concerning my class selections. In fact, I did not have the same enthusiasm concerning the arts and humanities classes. So, as you can see, I could rightfully claim that I am the originator of the STEM acronym. Well, I must admit that I did enjoy my history class because I had a passion for learning all I could about the United States history. Even at one point, my professor asked me if I was a history major and recommended a set of alternative history books.

Chapter 1

This was one of the times when I wish that I could be cloned many times over so that I could have attended multiple classes concurrently. It is quite apparent that my physical being has imposed limitations on my academic ambition. I wish that I could spread the passion I have for learning to everyone. Besides, wouldn't it be nice to have our society treat our academic scholars, whose efforts excel above their peers, the very way we treat our athletes and celebrities? Wouldn't it be a wonderful incentive to see our fellow outstanding classmates and professors being featured on products too? Most notably on the front of the Wheaties box and the packages of our popular children's products. Although I digress a little, the point I am conveying is that outstanding academic achievements should be recognized, valued, and perpetuated by all sectors of our society.

Okay, I should get back to the moment at hand. Finally, after a long but worthwhile wait, Mr. Wuollet was through teaching his class. Once again in a soft tone of voice, he said, "Please take a walk with me to my office." I did accordingly, and he spent approximately thirty to forty minutes going over the DMT program with me. He also went over the curriculum and the prerequisites. After he was through, I was convinced that this program would allow me to accomplish my goal of pursuing a degree in the electronics and computer technology field.

The real dilemma for me was how I would make the case to the college that I would like to transfer from the hospitality program to the DMT program. What would be the rationale for the sudden change regarding my major? Well, this should not have been a difficult undertaking, seeing that, for the past three years, I had worked for the

## Onward Bound to the United States of America

Airports Authority of Jamaica as an electrician. I was also on study leave and had to return to work in such capacity after I was through with my studies in the United States. Besides, pursuing a degree in the digital and microprocessor technology field would be more beneficial to both parties.

Justifying my decision proved to be a much easier undertaking than I had initially thought. I was very fortunate to have known one of the senior Jamaicans, Yvonne, who was working as a student aid with the dean's office. Actually, Yvonne and I were two of the first residential trainees to have graduated from the Runaway Bay HEART Academy Hotel Management training program. With that said, the following day I expressed my desire to her and, with no hesitation whatsoever, she said, "Small Boy, don't worry. I will talk with Mr. Wood for you." By the way, if you are curious as to why she addressed me as Small Boy, then please check out volume 3 of my autobiography, where you will uncover many hidden secrets. Anyway, she did just that and scheduled an appointment for me to discuss my program change with the dean.

With much anticipation, the day finally arrived, and it was time for me to explain my rationale to Mr. Wood. The minute I stepped into his office, he turned to me and said, "Why, after spending the first term in the hospitality program, have you decided to change your major?" I told him that I was on study leave from the Airports Authority of Jamaica, where I was currently working as an electrician and had to return to work in such capacity. I also explained to him that a DMT major would be more beneficial for both parties. After I was through explaining, Mr. Wood said, "From what I have heard, I do not see why you would not be allowed to pursue a degree that would be most beneficial to you and your current employer." He concluded by asking me to put my request in writing, which I did. And that was all it took for me to transfer from the hospitality program to the DMT program.

**Embarking on a New Academic Frontier**

At the end of the fall college term, I registered for my first four courses in the DMT program. To gain a much-needed advantage, I went ahead and purchased all the required textbooks and supporting materials before the start of the winter quarter. With the desired resources in hand, I spent much of the college break reading through the textbooks and prepping for the labs. This proactive measure was essential, especially knowing that I was definitely not a fast-paced learner. Also, this head start was vital because I was about to embark on an entirely new knowledge quest.

The fall term ended, and the winter term started with a bang. I found the courses to be very challenging, due to the overwhelming amount of information that I had to absorb in approximately three months. The many sleepless nights had paid big dividends, as indicated by my scorecard below. Once again, I was placed on the president's list.

1992 WINTER QUARTER

| COURSE | DESCRIPTION | IAI | CR HRS | HRS ATT | GR | HRS ERN | HON PTS | GPA |
|---|---|---|---|---|---|---|---|---|
| CIS 100 | INTRO COMPUTERS | | 4.00 | 4.00 | A | 4.00 | 16.00 | |
| DMT 101 | ELEC CIRC FUND | | 5.00 | 5.00 | A | 5.00 | 20.00 | |
| DMT 151 | SEMICONDUCTOR | | 5.00 | 5.00 | B | 5.00 | 15.00 | |
| MATH 118 | TECHNICAL MATH | | 4.00 | 4.00 | A | 4.00 | 16.00 | |
| QUARTER TOTALS | | | 18.00 | 18.00 | | 18.00 | 67.00 | 3.72 |
| CUMULATIVE TOTALS | | | 31.00 | 31.00 | | 31.00 | 114.00 | 3.67 |

34

## The Passing of My Father

My whole life was interrupted when I received the devastating news that my father had passed away. I was saddened by his passing because I had never had an opportunity to fulfill my dream of experiencing a father-son relationship. Or even to let him know that, regardless of our cultural and religious differences, he was my father and I cared deeply about his well-being. Although I did not succeed in such regard, I will always cherish the short but interesting memories of my father, as outlined in volume 1 of my autobiography. Knowing that I would never have the opportunity to speak with my father again has altered my psychological state concerning him.

## Back on Track

Despite the loss of my father, I had to recalibrate my mind back to my academic studies because time was of the essence. As time progressed, I adjusted to the pace and workload associated with the DMT program. However, just before I was through with the DMT program, I realized the importance of expanding my studies into the computer information systems field. With that in mind, I found myself exploring the possibilities associated with software development. My desire was further heightened when I saw Pragnesh, a friend and co-worker, working on several assignments from the computer information systems program. After a couple of questions in such regard, he took some time to explain the significance of the program and the benefits associated with becoming a software developer. After looking over his shoulder for a while, I was intrigued

## Chapter 1

by the level of sophistication that he was able to employ with the aid of high-level programming languages. I was very excited about the prospects for such knowledge back in Jamaica, especially with the Airports Authority. From that point forward, I told myself that I should not return to Jamaica without acquiring such knowledge. Once again, I scheduled an appointment with the dean.

Can you imagine what must have been going through Mr. Wood's mind when he got the message that I needed to speak with him again regarding my academic studies? He probably was saying to himself, "What does this Jamaican want from me? Haven't I done enough for him already?" Let me stop speculating and tell you exactly what happened. After pleading my case to Mr. Wood, he permitted me to enroll in the computer information systems program. However, I was not so fortunate from a financial perspective because I was unable to secure a tuition waiver. Therefore, in addition to my regular expenses, I was also responsible for the tuition associated with my second degree. My financial woes were compounded because the non-resident student tuition was a lot more expensive than that of the in-state tuition. Once again, the college never gave me more than I could bear. Mr. Wood pleaded on my behalf, and the college waved the non-resident portion of the tuition, thus making it affordable for me to pursue a second degree.

In March 1994, I graduated from the DMT program with high honors. This was my first graduation ceremony in the United States and, surely, it was a wonderful experience. What once had been merely a dream had finally become a reality. Undoubtedly, this achievement surpassed my wildest imagination.

Although I did not have any of my family members in attendance, it felt as though my entire family were present because Ed, his brother, David, and his sister-in-law, Rachel, were there to cheer me on. Rachel also baked a delicious cake to celebrate my first significant accomplishment in the United States of America. I have included a picture because this was no ordinary cake. In fact, it was homemade and was fully decorated with the colors black, green, and yellow, which symbolize the Jamaican flag. Also, it included the famous "Feeling Irie!" Jamaican quote. If you want to see the cake in full HD, then you will just have to navigate to my website (www.fosteringthroughtheeyesofachild.net). These are the acts of kindness that are not easily expressed with words because they have surpassed my human comprehension.

As you can see, I had my cake and ate a piece of it too.

I do not want to give the impression that I am the only one who should be credited for my academic success. In fact, had it not been for the DMT program coordinator, professor, mentor, and friend, Marty Wuollet, I can assure you that my academic undertaking would have been a lot more difficult. Mr. Wuollet was never too busy to assist me. In fact, there were times when I would show up at his office unannounced and, instead of chasing me away or reminding me that it was his lunch hour, he would say to me, "I tell you what, I can help you, but you will have to join me for lunch." With that said, we would walk to the cafeteria together, where I would discuss my problems and concerns with him over lunch. There were times when I found myself struggling because I did not understand a specific topic or lab assignment. However, with his keen sense of awareness, Mr. Wuollet would detect my frustration, walk right over to my desk, and, in a very calm and collected manner, say, "Don't be too hard on yourself. Come and see me after class." Most of the time, I was the cause of my problem but, nonetheless, Mr. Wuollet did not get frustrated. Neither did he give up on me.

Here is a typical example to substantiate the above claim as it pertains to Mr. Wuollet's patience and thoughtfulness. During one of my lab sessions, I was experiencing difficulties getting my circuit to work. Little did I realize that this was one of those "self-inflicted wound" situations. I was so taken up with the circuit design that I had totally forgotten to plug the power cord into the electrical outlet. Instead of making sure that the circuit was powered up, I resorted to all sorts of troubleshooting techniques. I wasted most of my lab time testing for open circuits, bad connectors, resistors, transistors, AND gates, OR gates, NAND gates, and BILL Gates. Oops, please disregard the last one—Bill Gates is not a microchip—but you get the point; I was looking for the problem in all the wrong places.

After spending almost an hour of the limited lab time on troubleshooting, it was time to turn over this problem to Professor Wuollet. I remember saying, "Mr. Wuollet, this thing does not work, and I did everything according to the book!" He looked up at me, knit his brow, and said, "Okay." Then he got up, approached my work area, and said, "Let me take a look." With one hand in his pocket and with the other stroking his chin (his trademark), he

## Onward Bound to the United States of America

said, "Aha! No matter how hard you try, nothing is going to happen. I can tell you why, but I will let you figure it out for yourself."

I became even more frustrated and started testing each and every component for a second time. Precious time was ticking away, so I beckoned to Mr. Wuollet and said, "Mr. Wuollet, I checked everything, and the circuit still does not work!" Instead of making a public announcement, he came over to my work table, leaned over and whispered, "Let me save you the embarrassment, because no matter how hard you try, the circuit is not going to work until you plug this into the outlet you see right here." Not only that, but making sure that the equipment was plugged in and powered up was one of the highlighted set of instructions outlined in the lab manual. Now you and I know why Mr. Wuollet knit his brow when I told him that I had done everything according to the book. If Mr. Wuollet had made a public announcement of my silly oversight, it would undoubtedly have become the subject of the class discussion for a very long time.

Before I proceed, I would like to share one last episode regarding my professor, Mr. Wuollet. One day while I was at work, I initiated a casual conversation with a young man who was sitting beside me. Other than this person being a schoolmate, I knew nothing else of him. Throughout our conversation, I spent most of the time talking about school (which I did 99.99 percent of the time), while bragging about my favorite professor. For some unknown reason, I did not refer to the professor by name. After I was through speaking highly regarding this professor, the young man asked, "What is the name of this professor you keep talking about?"

I replied, "Mr. Wuollet."

That was when the young man looked directly at me and said, "That's my dad."

At first, I thought he was kidding. However, I quickly realized that he was not kidding when he started to share more with me regarding his dad. This encounter was a true reflection of the saying, "If you do not have something good to say, then do not say anything at all." This also reminds me that people, such as Mr. Wuollet with compassionate hearts do not need spokespersons because the ones (persons like me) they care for will reflect the kindness that has been bestowed unto them.

Despite my inability to learn at the average pace, over the years I came to realize that effort and perseverance are the internal attributes that have contributed to my academic success. However, I have also learned that external factors, that include having thoughtful, understanding, caring, and trustworthy professor such as Mr. Wuollet, are the complementary motivators that facilitate academic success. For these reasons, I would like to take this moment to say a special thank you to my favorite professor, Mr. Marty Wuollet, for being a thoughtful and caring professor, mentor, and friend.

Each time that I reflect on my accomplishments, I cannot help but think of my only brother. I could envision my brother graduating from the College of DuPage or a similar institution if only he had caring and trustworthy people in his life.

## The Summer Heat

Once again, there was no rest for the weary, because it was time for me to commence my second associate of applied science (AAS) degree program. Even with the out-of-state portion of the tuition waived, I still had no idea how I would finance the remainder of the tuition. However, I did not let that stop me from moving forward. My first plan was to find a way to increase my earnings over the summer break. I needed to make sure that there was enough work in the janitorial department to keep me employed. With that in mind, I went to my supervisor, Cliff, and asked him if he would assign me the task of cleaning the rust from the windows over the summer. He looked at me and said, "I don't see why not." Then he went on to say, "Do you realize that those windows have been that way for many years, and we do not have any glass cleaner strong enough to clean them?" After hearing what Cliff had said, I realized that this would undoubtedly be a very daunting task because an entire section of the college exterior windowpanes was completely covered with rust stains.

## Job Creation Effort

Just like a chemist, I started out by applying several solutions to a small section of the window and let them sit for a couple of minutes before I washed them off. First I tried the strongest concentrated glass cleaner that was at my disposal, but that did not work. Second I tried WD-40, and that did not work well either. Third I tried a little oven cleaner, and it removed some of the rust, but I could see

## Chapter 1

that it needed a little scrubbing. With that in mind, I took a soft bristle pad and rubbed lightly over the area where I had applied the oven cleaner and, voilà, that was the solution. I cleaned the entire pane of glass, then hurried back to the janitorial office and summoned my supervisor to come and see my revolutionary breakthrough. After observing me clean another pane, he gave me the go-ahead to clean all the windows throughout that section of the college.

For the entire summer, I worked many hours, sometimes with the aid of my fellow student coworkers, scrubbing away many years of iron rust stains from the college windows. Cleaning those windows was the most challenging task I had undertaken since setting foot in the United States. Even to this day, I can still hear a "snap crackle pop" sound in my right shoulder whenever I perform a circular "wax on, wax off" motion.

Anyway, despite the tedious undertaking, I earned enough money to fund the first two terms of my computer information system (CIS) program. As soon as registration commenced, I went ahead and registered for my first term in the CIS program. Little did I realize how challenging and time-consuming four computer programming courses would turn out to be. They certainly kept me busy and made me realize that I needed more than twenty-four hours in my day.

Before I venture onto the next phase of my academic journey, I would like to share with you the final chapter of Jasmin Wynter's life. Ms. Wynter was the manager of the Runaway Bay HEART Academy and the person who had made it possible for me to embark on such a life-changing academic career in the United States of America. To put her in context, please refer to volume 3 of my autobiography. While pursuing my degree in the United States, I kept in touch with Ms. Wynter frequently. I used to inquire of her how she was doing and how the training program at the Runaway Bay HEART Academy was going. In addition to our casual conversations, I would fill her in on my academic progress at the College of DuPage and how I would like to use my acquired knowledge to contribute back to the academy and Jamaica as a whole. One day, just as I came home, my roommate presented me with one of the saddest and most gut-wrenching pieces of news one could ever imagine. She told me that Ms. Wynter had been involved in a terrible motor vehicle accident, and that she had passed away. I was devastated. I started questioning why something like this had to happen to such a wonderful person. It was very difficult for me to come to terms with this sad and painful situation. I could not understand why people of such warm and tender hearts had to pass away so soon. I had been really looking forward to meeting her in person again so that I could thank her for her overwhelming kindness and sincere generosity. I had been hoping that someday I could collaborate with her on some form of technology initiative to benefit the HEART Academy. Despite the bad news, I have learned to accept the fact that God is the only one who can provide clarity and comfort to our grieving souls. May her soul rest in peace.

CHAPTER 2

# GOING OUR SEPARATE WAYS

Just when I thought all was well, I was once again confronted with another major decision. My affordable living accommodation was coming to an end, but I did not have another comparable alternative. My roommates had accomplished their academic goals, and it was now time for us to go our separate ways. As for me, I had just started my second AAS degree program and needed to stick around for at least another year. Therefore, it was up to me to figure out what I was going to do about my living accommodation. With that said, one day I casually brought up the subject about needing a room to rent with my classmate Ed. We did not dwell on the subject because our conversation ended prematurely; however, it was enough to resonate in his mind.

Approximately a month before the lease on our apartment expired, Ed asked me if I was still looking for a place to rent. I had not yet found an apartment, so I replied with a resounding "Yes, I am!" He then asked if I would be interested in renting his two-bedroom townhouse. Without any consideration, I told him that I was only working part-time and was looking for something more affordable. He asked me how much I was currently paying, and I told him $165 per month, excluding utilities. I was surprised when he told me that he would rent me a room for $165 per month. I said to him, "This sounds like a generous offer, so what's the catch?"

He explained to me that he had gotten a job that would require him to be away from home for approximately two years, and he was more interested in having someone at his home that he could trust. He also told me that he was quite reluctant to leave his home unattended throughout the winter. He concluded the conversation by saying, "Desmond, I don't foresee any problem letting you stay at my home." Speaking from experience, I can affirm that the Chicago winters can be quite brutal, but I will let you know shortly if a Jamaican has what it takes to keep a home secure throughout the freezing Chicago winters. Anyway, after listening to Ed, I took a deep breath because this was yet another reminder that with God, all things are possible.

Finally, after all was said and done, my Jamaican roommates and I bid each other goodbye and went our separate ways. After a short reminiscing of the past two-plus memorable years that we had spent together, I took my belongings and hurried off to my new apartment. When I got there, Ed was just about to leave for his first out-of-state assignment, which meant that he had little time to discuss the details with me. However, earlier he had told me that, in his absence, I must consider his home my home. This arrangement could be classified as one of those "mi casa, su casa" arrangements. He left the Sunday afternoon of that week and promised that he would keep in contact to make sure everything was ok. As time progressed, Ed would come home on Fridays and leave again on Sundays.

As for my new accommodation, all was going well and I was enjoying every bit of it. I simply could not have asked for anything more. However, my overall expense was still a challenge. Although I had initiated many cost-saving measures throughout the first two years of my college career, it was in my final two years that I had to implement the most stringent budgetary constraints one could ever imagine. For example, I had to say goodbye to the recommended three meals per day and adopt the one- or maybe two-meal (if there were leftovers after a function hosted by the college) per day modified meal plan. I can assure you that working with a meager income forced me to budget every penny. This was the time that I wished I could have supplemented my budget by planting and selling vegetables. Well, that was a nonstarter idea because Chicago is certainly no place for a Jamaican farmer.

Nonetheless, that was it for the cost-cutting measures. Now let's see my progress as I traverse the computer information systems program. As for the more advanced programming classes, I would spend most of my available time at the college computer lab. Many nights after the lab was closed (10:00 p.m.), I would go by Rick's (a friend of mine) home and camp out in his basement, coding away on his computer for another three to four hours. Although it was cold and shivery in the basement, Rick would offset much of the cold by firing up a kerosene oil heater. Also, he would prepare a large pot of tea for me to sip on. Many times I would call on him for his help whenever I was unable to figure out why my "perfectly well thought-through" programming logic did not work as intended. Just to let you know, my code was never the problem, it was always the compiler complaining that there were errors.

Chapter 2

Another one of my study maximization efforts involved staying at home for most of the holidays. In fact, I used the holidays to catch up or, in some instances, to get ahead with my studies. However, I did make an exception for the major holidays such as the Fourth of July, Thanksgiving, and Christmas. That is, instead of staying home and spending those days on the computer, I would go by Ed's family, a professor, or a classmate's home, where I would enjoy Thanksgiving or other important get-together occasions.

**The Unforgettable Blizzard**

Everything was going great! Life was like having a "cool runnings" delicious ice cream topped off with lots of "no problem, man" sprinkles. College life was in full swing, and I was enjoying every minute of it. However, the good times were brutally disrupted on January 18, 1994, when the actual temperature dipped down to minus twenty-one degrees Fahrenheit! Believe me, my Jamaican brethren, when I tell you that the actual temperature was much colder than inside your freezers! Trust me, I have been through it and have lived to tell the tale.

I distinctly remember that the radio and television stations issued stern and repeated warnings that all residents should leave at least one faucet dripping inside the home to prevent the pipes from freezing. I remember leaving the kitchen faucet dripping before retiring to bed that night. However, I got up later that night, heard the faucet dripping, walked right into the kitchen, and turned it off without any consideration whatsoever! Who knows, I must have been exercising one of my many cost-saving

## Going Our Separate Ways

measures. Anyway, the next morning when I woke up, I went into the bathroom and turned on the faucet only to discover that there was absolutely no water coming from it. My first reaction was that probably something was wrong with the bathroom faucet. No problem, I would just have to fetch water from the kitchen. I went into the kitchen and turned on the faucet, but after seeing no water coming from it, I realized that I had made a big blunder. I had absolutely no running water inside the house. And to compound the issue, the central heating system was not working either.

I was quite fortunate that Ed had given me the homeowners association contact information. With that said, I contacted the office and explained the situation to the representative. She told me that the office would dispatch someone to the house right away. I waited and waited, but no one came. I went ahead and made a second call and then waited some more. Finally, after approximately three hours, I saw a vehicle pull into the driveway. I went downstairs, opened the door, and greeted the workmen with a pleasant good morning. However, they were in no mood for any courtesy gestures.

Moreover, the expression on their faces was a good indication that they were not there for any happy talk, either. How could I blame them? First, being out and about in twenty-degree-below-zero weather was certainly no fun for the average person, much less for workers summoned to thaw frozen pipes. Nevertheless, one of the men asked me if I were the owner of the house, and I told him no. I told him that I was the tenant and that the owner was out of town. He then replied in a very stern voice, "Did you not listen to the weather channel or the local news?" I said,

## Chapter 2

"yes." Then he said, "So why didn't you leave one of the faucets trickling!" Instead of answering his direct question, I replied by letting him know that I had just migrated from Jamaica and I had never experienced this type of weather before. Guess what, that Jamaican "pity story" bought me a little grace because they calmed down right away. After explaining the procedure and the risks associated with the thawing process, they went ahead and hooked up a heating device to the plumbing system.

For those of us who are not familiar with or have no experience living in a cold region, let me explain the risks that are associated with this pipe-thawing process. According to the workers, there is a high probability that the pipes could rupture due to excessive pressure, causing severe water damage to the drywalls throughout the house. In other words, there was a high probability that this thawing process could turn out to be an expensive undertaking. After they informed me of the disaster that could happen, I found myself under a lot more pressure than the frozen pipes. When they were through hooking up the heating device to the pipe, we conversed for a while, mostly about Jamaica. They asked what I was doing in Chicago and why I would ever consider leaving a warm, sunny, beautiful island such as Jamaica to come to a cold place like Chicago. Well, their concern was certainly not an isolated one because for the entire five years I spent in Chicago, I was asked that very same question many times over. As for me, education was the primary driving force, which I conveyed to them.

The thawing process was taking much longer than anticipated, so the workers left the device on the pipe and told me that they would be back shortly. I was freezing!

*Going Our Separate Ways*

And to make matters worse, I had no running water and was badly in need of a cup of tea. Having no clue when this thawing process would be completed, I took a one-gallon container and hurried across the street to see if my neighbor (a woman I had met briefly in the computer lab) would be kind enough to provide me with a gallon of water. I rang the doorbell several times, and she opened the door and greeted me with a pleasant good morning. I responded by singing the lyrics of Bob Marley's "Coming in from the Cold" song. Yeah right! It was so darn cold I could barely open my mouth.

Here is how the actual conversation transpired. I greeted the woman with a shivering good morning, then asked her to please spare me a gallon of water. She invited me inside and asked, "What happened to your water?" I told her that I had no water because the pipes were frozen. She asked me if there was heat in the apartment, and I told her no. Immediately, in a stern but caring voice, she said, "Do not go back inside that cold place. You can catch pneumonia and die!" Then she told me that I was welcome to stay at her place until the water and the heat were restored. I did not want to be of any inconvenience to her so, instead of sticking around, I thanked her for the water and went back home. I drank several cups of tea, but it appeared as though the more tea I drank, the colder I got. After sitting in the apartment for approximately thirty minutes, I decided to go back to the neighbor's home to take her up on her generous offer. Here is the truth: I was quite concerned when she told me that I could catch pneumonia and die.

With that in mind, I packed a little bag with some clothes and went back to the neighbor's home. The minute

## Chapter 2

I rang the bell, she opened the door and said, "I knew you would come back because if you stay in that house with no heat, you would certainly catch pneumonia." Then she said, "If you want to take a shower, you are more than welcome to do so." As soon as she directed me to the bathroom, I thanked her, ran upstairs, and took a long hot shower. When I was through showering, she had a large cup of hot chocolate waiting for me on the table. After chatting with her and her son for approximately one hour, I looked out the window and noticed that the workers had returned to the apartment to check if the pipes were thawed. I thanked the lady and hurried home, hoping and praying for good news. And that was exactly what I got. However, the workmen reminded me of how lucky I was, considering all the possibilities if the pipes had ruptured. I guess they had to rub it in one last time to make sure that I did not repeat this silly mistake.

Although this blunder could have been a lot worse, I want to point out that the thawing process did cost me a fortune with regard to my electric bill. I also realized that I needed to listen to the local news and weather channel, and take the necessary precautions whenever we were experiencing a major blizzard such as this one. After I got the hot water and the furnace up and running, I placed the thermostat at the highest level, hoping that within a couple of minutes the house would be at a livable temperature. Although the heater was at the highest level possible, it was still freezing cold in the apartment. Just to be on the safe side, I went back to the neighbor's home and camped out there for a while. Later that afternoon, I went back to the apartment, and as soon as I opened the door, I felt the gentle warm air flowing from the vents. Having experienced such a brutal Chicago winter, from that point forward, I made sure that I left not just one but two (the kitchen and the bathtub) faucets dripping, just in case I mistakenly turned off one or the other.

Here is a more realistic example that will further explain the devastating effects of the Chicago frigid temperatures and the unintended consequences associated with frozen pipes. A section of the McDonald's headquarter building located in Oakbrook, Illinois, was flooded when a rather large water main located on the roof ruptured during the thawing process. In other words, an exposed section of the pipe was frozen by the frigid temperature and as soon as the temperature started to rise the frozen pipe began to thaw, and the excessive pressure caused a section of the pipe to burst. To complicate the matter, the room that housed the most important technology equipment was also flooded. However, this disaster became an opportunity for me because I worked many hours on the technology recovery project. With that said, I should not be complaining about the Chicago blizzard too much. Moreover, the financial reward I received from the restoration project was a clear indication that out of disaster comes a little fortune.

As it pertains to Ed, if the outcome had resulted in burst pipes and excess flooding, then it would have taught him a valuable lesson to never again leave a Jamaican in charge of his property throughout the winter season. Before I continue, I would like to take a moment to say a big thank you to the wonderful, compassionate lady whose name should be rolling right off my tongue; but unfortunately, I cannot recall it because she left the neighborhood shortly after the blizzard. You will have to give me a pass because when I met her, I was experiencing a massive "brain freeze."

## Chapter 2

Hmmm, I wonder if she had enough of the Chicago frigid weather and migrated to Jamaica? Just a thought. Anyway, I am happy I did take a picture of her for keeps. And who needs a name when "a picture is worth a thousand words."³ Despite not remembering her name, I can assure you that her kindness and her overwhelming compassion were such that I will never forget. Please stay tuned because we are not yet through with this "frigid" episode.

Over the next couple of days, the temperature was still in the double digits below zero, so I decided that "home sweet home" was where I belonged. However, before I could get too comfortable, my supervisor contacted me and told me that I needed to report to work as soon as possible. I could not believe what I was hearing. From my perspective, my supervisor was kidding, or she was absolutely crazy? Doesn't an American realize that being outdoors in subzero temperature is considered suicidal for a Jamaican? Well, I guess if others were forced to brave the frigid cold, then so should I. With that said, I dressed in several layers of blizzard-resistant attire, looking as though I were getting ready to explore the North Pole.

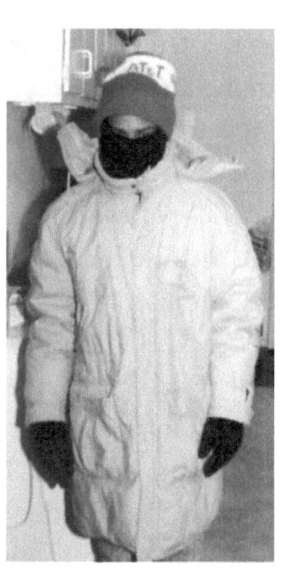

Now you know that Jamaican Eskimos do exist.

Most of the time, I would set out on foot because my unreliable Chrysler would fail to start, or sometimes it

---

3 See picture at *www.fosteringthroughtheeyesofachild.net*.

## Going Our Separate Ways

would start but would fail at the first intersection between point A and point B. However, that morning, I had no intention of walking to school! With that in mind, I gave the old Chrysler a couple of cranks and finally! the engine started. The engine revved at a very high RPM and sounded as if it were about to explode. Nonetheless, I got it going. However, the short journey turned out to be the bumpiest ride I had ever had! I felt as though I were being dragged around on a solid hunk of metal. Despite the bumpy ride, I made it to the college without the car failing or falling apart. Upon arrival, I was shocked to see so many vehicles in the college parking lot! I thought that only a handful of people would have dared to venture out into the frigid cold, but once again, I was wrong. The real question was who were these professors and students, and why were they so dedicated to a cause? I mean, not even the double-digit freezing temperature was able to stop or slow down these brave academic explorers. Anyway, I navigated through the frozen parking lots until I found a close enough parking space. After parking, I made a mad dash across the parking lot and into the building. I was delighted to be out of that brutal, unbearable weather!

After I was through working that afternoon, I went to my car and, lo and behold, the unthinkable had happened! My front tires appeared to have been deflated through a process known as deflate-gate. This posed a significant challenge for me because there was absolutely no way that I was going out in a double-digit subzero temperature to change flat tires. Nor was I ever contemplating walking home either. Instead, I decided that I would drive to the closest gas station and put air in the tires. If you think that the ride I had on my way to work that morning had

## Chapter 2

been rough, then I say think again. The one I had on my way to the gas station was the most horrible car ride I ever had. Even a Jamaican handcart provides a more comfortable ride than a ten-ton frozen Chrysler with deflated tires.

Despite the uncomfortable ride, I made it to the gas station safely. However, just as I was going up the little slope toward the air pump, my car got stuck on a big patch of ice. I made several unsuccessful attempts to get it going, but the wheels kept turning but could not get any traction. I could not go forward or backward. There I was, approximately seventy-five feet away from the air pump but could not get any closer. After many unsuccessful attempts, a man saw my frustration, came over to where I was, and asked, "Are you ok?" I told him that my car was stuck, and I was unable to move in any direction. He then asked me if I had any crushed stones in my car. I had no idea why he posed such a question because if the weight was a factor, then I certainly did not need another pound because the old Chrysler by itself weighed as much as a fully loaded semitrailer truck. Not quite, but close. Anyway, seeing that I was actually freezing to death and certainly did not have the time or the energy for humor, I told him that I did not have any crushed stones in the car. He then walked back to his car and retrieved a bag of crushed stones. He told me to put the car in drive and slowly accelerate while he threw some of the stones before the front wheels.

We repeated the process several times until I made it to the air pump. What a relief! I thanked the gentleman several times for his generosity. Before leaving, he turned to me and said, "I detect an accent, where are you from?" I replied, "Jamaica." Then he said, "Let me give you a list of things you need to have in your car throughout the winter." I was not too interested in hearing about his list because I had made up my mind that this was my last winter in Chicago. But, nonetheless, I listened. Although I do not remember the complete list, here is what I can recall from memory: two bags of crushed stones, a blanket or sleeping bag, a pair of snow boots, cap, scarf, jacket, gloves. Once again, I expressed my gratitude to him; then he wished me safe travel and drove off. By the way, please let me know if I have omitted any essential life-saving items from the above list.

Okay, time to get some air in the tires and head on home. By the time I got to the air pump, I could not feel any life in my fingers. I simply could not remove or unscrew the caps from the air valves. After discovering that I was unable to put any air in the tires, I decided that, flat tires or not, I was going home. Although it was one of the most uncomfortable rides I ever had, I made it home safely. Upon arrival, I pressed the garage door opener (lucky for me, I did not have to use a key). As soon as the garage door was up high enough, I dashed underneath it, opened the door to the stairway, rushed upstairs, swung the faucet handle to the hot position, and placed my hands underneath it.

Within a couple of seconds, I felt an excruciating pain radiating through my fingers. It felt as though I were being poked with a thousand needles. I kept my hands under the water while asking the Lord to restore life to my fingers. I was quite worried when I found that I could barely move my fingers. With that in mind, I started thinking about what it would be like if I were unable to pursue my academic and professional career. After a while,

## Chapter 2

I started feeling the life being restored to my fingers. It started out with one finger, then another and another, until life was fully restored to all my fingers. After sensation was restored to my fingers, I was the happiest person alive that day! It was a hallelujah moment for me when I was able to move my fingers freely and pick up objects. It is undoubtedly a very frightening experience to lose feeling to a member of your body, especially your fingers. This experience reminded me to be more appreciative of the little things in life that I take for granted; one of which was having the ability to move my fingers and to be able to pick up an object.

The moment life was restored to my fingers, I took the phone directory and retrieved the phone numbers for Air Jamaica and American Airlines. However, after dialing both airlines, I discovered that the cheapest airfare was somewhere in the price range of $750, which was entirely out of my affordable range. Either everyone was leaving town, or the airlines viewed this as an opportunity to maximize profits. That day I came to realize that my hope of booking a one-way ticket back to the warm and sunny island of Jamaica was never going to be realized. Therefore, not having the money meant that I had no other choice but to bundle up and ride out the cold, just like everyone else. Remember the dream I had in which I saw many young fruits that symbolized hardship? Well, I do believe I had just gotten my first shipment of frozen mangoes. Although I had suffered many hardships throughout my childhood, I would like to emphasize that no Jamaican hardship could ever have prepared me for the Chicago frigid temperatures! To further prove my point, I have included a snap-chart with January's 1994 recorded temperatures.

*Going Our Separate Ways*

### 1994 - Temperatures (F) Recorded in Chicago

```
  0
 -5
-10        15-Jan    16-Jan    18-Jan    19-Jan
-15
                      -16
-20        -17
                                          -19
                                -21
-25
```

Source Data: National Weather Service
http://www.weather.gov/lot/Chicago_Temperature_Records

## Frozen Fruits

Despite the brutal and scary winter, I was very fortunate to have had a successful first term in the computer information system program. Now I truly understand the well-known phrase that states, "When the going gets cold, the cold get going." That's not quite how it goes, but I simply could not resist. Please see my transcript below.

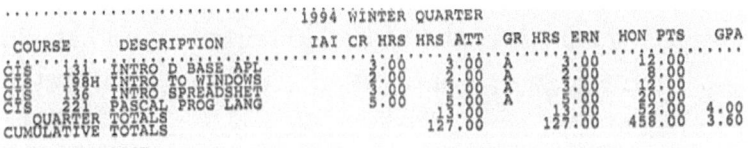

## The Enormous Expenditure

The outcome of the first term gave me a boost of confidence that propelled me through the rest of the program. Irrespective of the first term's success, I quickly realized that I needed a personal computer to complete the more

## Chapter 2

advanced programming courses. Besides, I needed to spend a lot more time on my programming assignments. However, the real question for me was where I would find the additional funds to purchase a computer; the average computer was around two thousand dollars at the time. My first step was to say goodbye to my little old Chrysler and say hello to my "foot mobile." With that said, I sold my car for a very large sum of money, which I would rather not disclose to the public. Well, on second thought, I might as well let you know that through a hard-fought negotiation with a Mexican buyer, I received a whopping $150 for my most unreliable Chrysler. The 150 you are seeing is not a typo.

Nonetheless, I did not miss that car because it was mostly at the college parking lot anyway. I remember one day while I was fiddling around trying to get the engine started, one of the college security guards came over to see if I needed help. The minute he approached the car, he asked, "Is this your car?" To which I replied, "Yes, it is." Then he said, "It seems like this car spends more time in the parking lot than at your home." We both had a good laugh because he was absolutely right. In fact, there were many cold days when it would not start, and I would ask a friend for a ride or just walk away, leaving it in the parking lot.

Anyway, now that I had taken this quantum financial leap forward, all I needed was a few smaller steps to attain another $1,850. It was necessary for me to take these measures because the little part-time job I had was my only source of income. For me to earn the remainder of the funds toward a computer, I needed to work twice as many hours or find a way to convince my manager that I needed a substantial increase. Well, it was obvious that the substantial increase prospect was a non-starter.

However, I was very fortunate because, in the summer of that year, the janitorial department provided me with the opportunity to work full time. I worked forty hours per week doing all sorts of janitorial work. Although I was quite exhausted at the end of the summer, I was extremely happy knowing that I had earned enough money to afford my first personal computer (PC). Wasting no time, Ed and I went shopping for a computer. After browsing, calculating, and comparing several brands and models of computers, I finally found an Acer brand with a price tag that was a little over two thousand dollars. Well, the price tag was a bit deceiving because I found out that the sticker price did not include taxes. I had absolutely forgotten that Uncle Sam needed a slice of the cake too. Not having enough money to pay the taxes, I decided to bargain with the cashier for a discount. However, she would neither "bit" nor "byte." Ed overheard the conversation and intervened, saying, "I know how hard you worked all summer for this computer, and I am not going to let you walk out of the store without it, so let me help you out." He was not kidding. He provided me with the needed funds and bought me a printer as well. At the time, excluding tuition and books, the computer was the largest single investment I had made toward my academic career.

Shortly after purchasing my first computer, I bought several programming books and development (programming) software from vendors at the local computer shows. So, after configuring my computer with all the necessary development tools, I spent many sleepless nights on the computer learning the art of programming. Sometimes

## Chapter 2

I would be on the computer from 8:00 p.m. to 8:00 a.m. without even taking a single cat nap. I had a passion for anything and everything related to computer technology. Having a high-powered computer at my fingertips made learning a lot more interesting. I was destined to become the most revered software programmer who ever walked the face of this earth. Well, so much for that dream because today, I am fortunate to be walking the face of the earth.

Okay, back to my knowledge quest. One of my most sought-after passions was to learn as much as I could so that upon my return to Jamaica, I could disseminate such knowledge through teaching and on-the-job training. Also, I was hoping that it would be possible for me to automate many of the operational tasks throughout the Donald Sangster International Airport. I was not sure how I would accomplish all these ambitious goals but, nonetheless, they acted as motivators for my never-ending knowledge quest. When I came to realize the endless potential that exists in the technology sector, I was wondering why Jamaica as a whole had not adopted a proactive approach toward building a vibrant computer information technology sector. Had it not been for the lack of vision, I strongly believe that Jamaica could have become the Silicone Island of the Caribbean.

Here is an example to support my claim as it pertains to the lack of vision that existed in Jamaica at the time. Throughout one of my visits to Jamaica, Mr. Tyson (my supervisor and academic mentor) asked me to purchase a computer for him so that he could use it to complete his college projects and other academic-related studies. However, I had a difficult time clearing customs due to the exorbitant duty that was levied on a personal computer. In this context, the Jamaican system valued short-term gains at the expense of long-term, long-lasting academic growth and development. Even to this day, I am still disturbed by the absence of noteworthy policies in such regard. To paraphrase the well-known proverb, where there is a lack of vision, a nation will inevitably suffer. It took almost a decade later for the government of Jamaica to realize the importance of this technology and implement a new policy that allowed an individual to bring in a personal computer as a duty-free item. However, the failure over those years severely impeded growth and development within the technology sector. Okay, I wandered off a little too deeply into Jamaica, so I will now get back to Chicago and take care of some unfinished business.

I must admit that there were times when I did a little too much regarding my projects, especially those associated with the use of a computer. One of my instructors, Diane, would say to me on several occasions, "Desmond, why are you putting so much pressure on yourself? You have done more than is required of you." Even a number of my peers would, at times, say to me, "Desmond, why do you spend so much of your time studying?" Here is the reason for my academic passion. To be the only child among my siblings to attend college was beyond my wildest imagination.

Furthermore, I have firsthand experience of what it is like for a child (including my siblings and me) to have missed out on his or her early childhood education. In addition, I also wanted to make Aunt Lucy (my foster mother) proud. It was always a joy to communicate my academic progress to her. Opportunity maximization was and still is my motto and one that I would like to encourage everyone to practice. My message to everyone, especially the younger generation, is this: Please find someone or something that gives you the drive and the determination you need to succeed, even if you seek a higher level of education and career aspiration than that of your parents. As long as you pursue your goals with humility, then I am quite sure that your parents, friends, or even strangers would not envy or deny you their full support.

**Low-Skill to High-Tech**

After working as a janitor for two-plus years, I decided to transfer from the janitorial department to the computing and information technology department. I worked as a part-time computer lab tech while completing the computer information systems degree program requirements, which was a big boost for my academic career.

**Off to the Sunny Island of Jamaica**

Just before I completed my final set of classes toward my computer information system degree, I took a surprise trip to Jamaica so that I could share my academic accomplishments with Aunt Lucy. With that said, on March 18, 1995, I booked a flight and off I went to the sunny island of Jamaica. Upon arrival, I drove with much haste to the little farming district of Sawyers. The minute I arrived, I shared with Aunt Lucy the exciting updates concerning my academic accomplishments. I could see the joy, the smile, and the happiness radiating from her face. We talked and shared wonderful memories together. She reminded me that my accomplishments had been made possible because of the wonderful blessings of God. As

I sat there, I found myself reminiscing on the day when my only hope had been for her to provide me with food and shelter in exchange for manual labor. Never in my wildest dreams had I ever imagined that what had been just a dream would someday become a reality. However, Aunt Lucy's overwhelming compassion led her to believe that my needs were far more than just the basic food and shelter I had asked of her.

On this trip, I also had the opportunity to be reunited with my only brother, George. Although his physical and psychological being was far different from the brother I had once known, deep down, I could sense that he was a lot more upbeat when compared to the last time we had met, which had been approximately ten years previously. However, it broke my heart to hear others addressing him as a mad or insane person. Especially those who were not familiar with his childhood physical and psychological struggles. He was no longer a Rastafarian. He had trimmed off his locks and was no longer adhering to our father's Rastafarian doctrine. However, he had not given up the marijuana smoking.

He and I drove from Montego Bay to Westmoreland to visit our mother. While on our way to Westmoreland, we talked about life in general. Knowing what my brother had been through while living with our former foster parents, I refrained from having any conversation that would take us back to that dark chapter. George did not make any reference to that period either. He was so happy to see me. He even asked me to stop the car on several occasions so that he could introduce me to acquaintances. He also introduced me to his favorite roadside restaurant and purchased a cup of peanut soup for me. He provided me with the rationale for why I needed to drink the peanut soup: "Drink dis mi bredda, it wi bill up yuh structure." ("Drink this, my brother, it will build up your body.") Well, he was onto something because I was very meager. Okay, I would not have been that skinny had it not been for Chicago's freezing weather.

Anyway, we finally made it to our mother's home. Even though our mother did not greet us as her sons or express any emotional bond toward us, we did have a friendly discussion with her. Later that evening, I bid goodbye to my mother and brother, then commenced my journey back to Montego Bay. The following day I went to the United States Embassy in Kingston and renewed my visa. Renewing my student visa was essential because I might have the need to continue with my knowledge quest. After my memorable return-to-the-island trip had ended, I boarded a flight back to the United States of America.

## The Final Stretch of My College of DuPage Academic Journey

At the end of the first phase of my academic journey in the United States, I was able to reap the rewards in the form of a second AAS degree as a computer information system/microcomputer specialist. I graduated with high honors and became a member of the Phi Theta Kappa honor society. After spending approximately four years at the College of DuPage and completing 171 credit hours that spanned hotel management, microprocessor technology, and computer information systems, it was now time for me to move on. See the transcript summary below.

```
REQUIREMENT OF SENATE BILL 195 MET
CERTIFICATE AWARDED:      06/13/93 MICROCOMPUTER SERVICING TECHNICIAN
CERTIFICATE AWARDED:      06/13/93 DIGITAL & MICROPROCESSOR TECH
DEGREE REQUIREMENTS MET:  03/20/94 ASSOCIATE IN APPLIED SCIENCE
                                   DIGITAL MICROPROCESSOR TECHNOLOGY
CERTIFICATE AWARDED:      03/19/95 MICROCOMPUTER SOFTWARE
CERTIFICATE AWARDED:      03/19/95 C PROGRAMMING LANGUAGE CERTIFICATE
DEGREE REQUIREMENTS MET:  06/11/95 ASSOCIATE IN APPLIED SCIENCE
                                   MICROCOMPUTER SPECIALIST
........................ 1995 SPRING QUARTER
COURSE      DESCRIPTION          IAI CR HRS HRS ATT  GR HRS ERN  HON PTS   GPA
ACCOU 151   PRINCIPLES I             4.00  4.00  A     4.00      16.00
CIS   110   MICRO DBAS D O S         5.00  5.00  A     5.00      20.00
     QUARTER TOTALS                        9.00        9.00      36.00    4.00
CUMULATIVE TOTALS                        171.00      171.00     616.00    3.80
```

Although I had endured many sleepless nights, it was all worth the pain for the academic gain. My accomplishments can be attributed to the undeserved blessings of God, my compassionate and loving foster mother (Aunt Lucy), and the sacrifices made on my behalf by my professors, mentors, and friends. Finally, I would like to acknowledge the faculty and staff members of the College of DuPage for extending unto me a warm welcome and for providing me with the keys to academic success. However, none of this would have been possible if I had not recognized that this was a once-in-a-lifetime opportunity and treated it as such. Just another reminder for the younger generation that you should always be grateful for the sacrifices that others have made on your behalf. Likewise, always strive to perpetuate the sacrifices of others, no matter how small or how insignificant they may appear to be.

Now that I had completed my studies at the College of DuPage, it was time for me to pack my bags and return to the tropical island of Jamaica. However, instead of going back to Jamaica as planned, I started contemplating the idea of attending a four-year college. With that

## Chapter 2

said, I decided to put my thoughts into action and started researching the costs. My search revealed the obvious; that is, attending a four-year college was simply not financially feasible. Well, at least that was my own understanding, but shortly after that, the Lord provided a way for me to earn a good portion of the funds toward my four-year college.

Here is how this golden opportunity came to fruition. One day I decided that it would be a good idea to have a little chat with my international student advisor. Throughout our conversation, he said, "Now that you are through with your associate degree, are you planning on pursuing your bachelor's degree?" I told him that I would like to but, unfortunately, it was not financially feasible. He followed up by saying, "Although it is not a good idea to apply for your practical training before completing your bachelor's degree, in this situation, I would suggest that you do so as a way to earn something toward your college expenses." And that was when I saw the light at the end of the tunnel.

The following day I went back to the International Student Affairs office to finalize the practical training process. It was not that easy because, as part of the process, I needed to obtain a work permit from the Immigration and Naturalization Service (INS) located in the heart of downtown Chicago. Once again, I was very fortunate because I contacted Rick, and he provided me with a ride to the INS office. That very day, I received my work permit and was ready to start earning some much-needed funds toward my four-year college.

Back then, information technology (IT) professionals were in high demand. Therefore, I did not have to send out a single résumé. Aren't we all yearning for the

1990s IT job explosion to come back? Okay, no time to dwell on yesterday, so let's get back to the day while I was sitting in the computer lab, refining my programming skills. There I was, minding my own business, when all of a sudden a man (an Aerotek engineering staffing firm recruiter) came over and sat beside me. In a very soft, whispering voice, he said, "Hello. Do you know of anyone who is currently looking for IT work?" He was whispering because he knew that he was in violation of the college's no soliciting policy. Anyway, one conversation led to the next, and he gave me one of his business cards, just in case I needed to contact him. Although I had been hoping for a software developer (programmer) job, I was a bit curious to hear more regarding this tech support job. With that said, I went ahead and contacted the recruiter, Tim, and he scheduled an interview with the company on my behalf. After the first interview, I was offered the job, which I accepted. However, I found out that I needed reliable transportation. With that in mind, I purchased a Ford Taurus from my friend, Michael, and hoped and prayed that it was not another Chrysler.

**Practical Training**

After the necessary requirements were completed, I commenced my one-year practical training with Palindrome (a software development company) as a technical support specialist. Everything was going great until Seagate Software acquired the company and outsourced most of the support operation. However, seeing that I was a contractor, I contacted Tim and asked him for a job reassignment, which he arranged. I worked as an IT consultant for Aerotek for the duration of my practical training. Throughout such time, I was very fortunate to have worked for several large corporations, which included Palindrome Corporation/Seagate Software, IBM/Advantis, McDonald's corporate headquarters in Oak Brook, Illinois, and Lucent Technologies' division in Naperville. These assignments allowed me to gain a tremendous amount of information technology experience.

## Clash of Religion and the Cultural Norms of Society

Just before I was through with my practical training, I was faced with a situation that cut across the very grain of my cultural beliefs and religious faith. This experience is not easy for me to discuss or rationalize because I do understand that everyone has his or her own opinion and even, at times, radical beliefs concerning religious norms and doctrines. However, this experience humbled me and gave me a different perspective with regard to the way I once perceived others who did not share the same beliefs and lifestyle choices. Concerning marriage and relationships, my cultural and religious beliefs and practices defined how and what I perceived to be the acceptable norm. In fact, I was taught that attraction, intimate friendship, and marriage concerning the opposite sex were considered the norm, and anything outside of this practice or lifestyle was considered a gross deviation from the norm of society and biblical principles. By the way, this is not only a religious doctrine; it is also a social doctrine that is valued by the Jamaican society as a whole. So there I was, faced with a decision in which I was caught up between my friendship, my culture, and my religious faith.

Before I explain why I am writing about this experience, I need to provide more insight regarding the subject of my conversation.

As time progressed, Ed and I became good friends. In addition to providing me an economical place to live when I was in need, he introduced me to his family, including his mother, father, brother, sister-in-law, nieces, and nephews. Occasionally, he would invite me to join him and his family for Thanksgiving and other get-togethers as a way of allowing me to take a break from my academic workload. At first, I was not too interested because I had laid out my study plan, and taking breaks for socializing was never an option on my busy agenda. However, after thinking it over, I decided to put the books aside and join him at his brother's or parents' home for Thanksgiving, watching the Soccer World Cup competitions, or for the Fourth of July celebration. I would like to extend my sincere thanks and gratitude to David and Rachel (Ed's brother and sister-in-law) for treating me like family, especially throughout Thanksgiving and other memorable family events. They also attended my first graduation ceremony in the United States; not to mention the lovely cake (the one I highlighted earlier), that Rachel baked for me.

Now that I have given you a synopsis of Ed and his family, I will outline the revelation that cut against the very core of my beliefs. Approximately three months before completing my practical training, I encountered a situation that I was surely not prepared for. Ed and I shared one computer, and, on several occasions, I would notice that the internet browser history contained information regarding gay social events and other gay-related information. At first, I did not think anything of it because it takes

## Chapter 2

a lot for me to start assuming or to arrive at any conclusion regarding a person's lifestyle. Moreover, at the time, I was way too busy with my studies to be concerned about anyone's personal life. However, based on my many discoveries, I suspected that Ed was either gay or was a gay rights activist. I decided to pose the question to him.

One morning, after we were through with breakfast, I asked, "Ed, are you gay?" He hesitated for a moment, then replied yes. Immediately, I went into a judgmental mode because I was not about to have my ego and my "righteousness" marred by Ed's lifestyle. The only thing left for me to do that morning was to reignite the Sodom and Gomorrah furnace. I was the first to cast stones (metaphorically) and lots of them too. The real question is this: What would have caused me to act in such a manner? Why did my natural instinct take over, and I did not realize it? Well, remember how I explained earlier that growing up in Jamaica, intimate relationships among the same sex were considered to be outside the norm. And how Ed would have been labeled a "battyman" and not a person you would want to be seen or to be associated with. With that said, I was ready to walk out the door and never return.

However, after I was through scolding, chastising, rebuking, and casting judgment, I asked Ed why he had kept this hidden from me all this time. Instead of getting upset, he replied calmly and said, "Desmond, I know you are a Christian, and I did not want to upset you."

I was a bit curious because I had never mentioned directly to Ed that I am a Christian. Only when warranted, I would quote a verse or two from the Bible or let him know that if it were not for the grace of God, I would not be the person I am. Nonetheless, I asked, "How could you say that I am a Christian when I had never told you that I am?"

Immediately, Ed replied, "Desmond, you did not have to tell me, it is quite obvious that you are." He also stated that, based on what he had seen and what I had told him, he knew that I was in the United States to fulfill my academic dream and he did not want his personal life to deny me such opportunity.

Despite having known Ed as a respectable person for over two years, I became overly sensitive and started to display a sense of uneasiness after discovering his lifestyle. Ed realized that I was never the same, so he sat me down for an in-depth conversation to quell the uneasiness. He told me that he had the utmost respect for me and that I should not think of him any less simply because of his lifestyle. Finally he told me that if I felt uncomfortable being around him and decided to leave, he would understand.

However, the Lord opened my eyes and made me realize that my behavior did not exemplify the humility or teachings of our Lord and Savior Jesus Christ. Nor did it reflect the very least of how a rational person should behave in this or a similar situation. I had allowed my ego, self-righteousness, and arrogance to take precedence over humility and commonsense-understanding. Neither did I seek the Lord's guidance as to what this revelation meant. Instead, I immediately saw myself as a "righteous" person who had been wrongfully placed among sinners.

Moreover, I should have known better because I had witnessed the physical and psychological harm suffered by the children who had been placed in my former foster parents' care. The children's suffering was a direct result of their ego and self-righteous persona. Not only that, but their self-righteousness caused me to adopt a cynical view of those who professed as though they had been given the authority to judge, to condemn, and to deny others the very gift of salvation. Now I found myself directing the same behaviors toward Ed. Which is why, today, I am very grateful that this experience reminded me that those of us who profess Christianity should not act as though we have been given dominion over our fellow humankind. Instead, we need to remind ourselves that others are entitled to the same grace, salvation, and forgiveness that God has bestowed unto us freely and in abundance. This revelation taught me much humility. I also realized that, instead of casting judgment on others, I should be asking God and my fellow humankind for forgiveness as it relates to my many transgressions.

    I seemed to have forgotten that I had known Ed as a person, a study partner, and as a friend long before his lifestyle was revealed to me. Although we differ regarding our lifestyles and our beliefs, that should by no means sever our communication, nor should it drive a wedge between us as human beings. I do believe that we should be ready and willing to forgive, to minister, and to have open and honest dialogs with our fellow humankind and leave all judgment to God. Moreover, if I decided to encircle myself with only those who think and act as I do, then I would surely be the only person occupying my "righteous circle." Little did I realize how arrogant I had become! How true is the scripture when it proclaims, "None is righteous, no, not one" (Romans 3:10, ESV). So let everyone examine his or her own life based on his or her own conscience. With such a humbling experience, I decided to start the conversation over with Ed; and this time, humility taught me how to communicate.

*Going Our Separate Ways*

## Is University Possible?

Approximately two weeks before the completion of my practical training, I was able to save a total of 10,500 dollars towards my bachelor of science degree. However, after conducting many hours of extensive research on the colleges located in the Chicago area, I found out that it was just not economically feasible, especially when taking into account the international or out-of-state tuition cost. With that said, I packed my belongings and bid my neighbors and friends goodbye. This was a mixed emotion for me because I had a burning desire to complete my bachelor's degree. However, I was happy to be going back home to Jamaica, especially knowing that I had acquired two associate (AAS) degrees and several certifications. Besides, I was excited to be going home to spend quality time with my family, especially Aunt Lucy. Also, I was happy to be finally getting away from the frigid Chicago temperatures.

## Could I Work Just a Little Longer?

However, Tim, my recruiter from Aerotek Engineering, interrupted my going-home mission with an irresistible proposition. He told me that based on my outstanding work ethic, he would like to look into the possibility of extending my work permit. I was very excited because being given the opportunity to work at least another year would provide me with the funds to finance my undergraduate degree. Unfortunately, after working for another two months, Tim told me that I needed to have at least a bachelor's degree for his company to petition on my behalf.

## Chapter 2

With that said, I had no other choice but to proceed with my back-to-Jamaica plan, but the delay provided me with the opportunity to save an additional two thousand dollars for my college expenses.

However, before I could get going with my back-to-Jamaica trip, a significant event caused me to revisit my going-to-college possibility one more time. Once again, what transpired is a living testimony that my life has never ceased to bear witness of God's astounding grace. It all started while I was at Lucent Technologies, completing my final week on the job. That day I received a call from Michael, my former College of DuPage roommate. He was then residing in Florida and attending Florida Atlantic University. I remember he started the conversation by saying, "My yout, mi have some good news fi yuh my yout." ("My friend [or brethren], I have some good news for you.") He followed up by saying, "My yout, FAU offa tuition discount if yuh have a good GPA." Without getting into the granular of our conversation, what Michael was saying was that the Florida Atlantic University was currently waving the out-of-state portion of the tuition for students and potential students with GPAs of at least 3.2 or higher. After acknowledging that I met the GPA requirement, Michael went ahead and filled me in on the financial details. I was sitting at the computer, so I brought up Excel and plugged in the numbers.

After analyzing the costs, I found out that I needed to have a minimum of $17,500 to cover the basic costs, including tuition. Knowing that I only had $12,500 on hand, I told Michael that I was unable to proceed based on the cost. However, he followed up by saying, "Yout, yuh can get a part-time job with the college to make up the

## Going Our Separate Ways

difference." He also told me that he worked for the registration department and would do everything possible to expedite the application process. Finally, he told me that he would inquire if there were any available student aid jobs with the university's computing and information systems department.

After listening to what Michael had to say, I started to feel a lot more confident, knowing that I was one step closer to extending my academic dream. In other words, it was highly probable that attending a four-year college was within reach. I needed to act quickly because my application should have been submitted several weeks before our conversation, which meant that time was of the utmost importance. With no further hesitation, I told Michael that I was interested and that he should proceed with the application process. He then instructed me to request a copy of the application forms, fill them out, and submit them to the university along with a copy of my unofficial transcript. He also outlined the necessary immigration requirements and the forms that I needed to complete in such regard. Surely, it was a big advantage to have Michael working on my behalf. He had all the inside "intel" and was able to remove the hiccups, which, in turn, sped up the process significantly. It was like having my own adviser to pave the way for me.

As soon as I got off the phone, I went to the College of DuPage and requested two copies (official and unofficial) of my transcript. I decided that, instead of staying in Illinois, I would relocate to Florida to expedite the application process. This was not an easy decision. That weekend I barely got any sleep, because I found myself contemplating two possibilities. First, to either fulfill my desire to go back

## Chapter 2

home to be with my family, especially my foster mother. Or second, to continue with my dream by embarking on yet another ambitious phase of my academic journey.

After a whole weekend of contemplation, I finally made up my mind that I was relocating to Florida to continue my academic dream. Although there were many reasons to be concerned, I was confident that everything would be just fine if I only accepted the known and left the unknown in the hands of God. Once I had made up my mind, it was time for me to move forward.

I had little time to get things together so, without further delay, I started packing away my belongings. In addition to my clothes and computers, I also packed several boxes of textbooks and technology-related books that I had accumulated over the past five and a half years. Rick, my friend, came by to assist me with my packing and noticed that I was loading several boxes of books into my car. With his quick insight, he said, "You are not planning on hauling all those books in your car to Florida?" I told him that I was planning on doing just that to save on shipping costs. That was when he said, "No! You do not want to do that! You are going to burn much more fuel that way. You need to ship them via UPS." He did not need to say another word because I was fully convinced. With that said, we packed the boxes into his van and took them to the UPS shipping depot.

The UPS attendant was a bit curious and asked, "Why are you shipping so many boxes of books to Florida? Everyone goes to Florida for vacation, but you are going there with a lifetime supply of books." Well, it was not exactly a lifetime supply of books because most of the computer-related books became obsolete in less than four years.

## Going Our Separate Ways

Nonetheless, we had a good laugh because when compared to the average person, I did possess quite a lot of books.

After I had every square inch of my car packed with clothes, computers, and other personal belongings, I was finally ready to take on a new frontier and "to boldly go" where I had never gone before. The irony of the situation was that I had never driven more than approximately fifty miles in any given direction from my home, so I was definitely in need of another miracle to help me cover this one-thousand-plus-mile journey. And once again, God provided Craig, who was a friend and a coworker, to escort me to a Florida location that was approximately fifteen miles north of my actual destination.

This miracle unfolded while Craig and I were indulging in one of our regular work-related conversations. He told me that he was in the process of transferring from the Lucent Technologies division in Illinois to another division located in Florida. The good news got even better when he told me that he was also relocating to Florida the following week! However, the best part of the conversation was when he told me that he was also driving to Florida. Not only that, but he also said that his destination was just a couple of miles north of mine. We could even carpool had it not been for all the bangarang I was transporting in my car. Nonetheless, I would like to say emphatically that this outcome was certainly not a coincidence! This was like having all the stars aligned in my favor. I was not sure if Craig knew how to get to Florida, so I asked him if I should purchase a road atlas just in case we needed it. He looked directly at me, smiled, and said, "No need to worry about any road atlas because I have done this journey many times before, and I could literally do it in my sleep." Immediately

## Chapter 2

after hearing such a bold statement, I breathed a sigh of relief, and my fear of driving from Illinois to Florida disappeared. I was overwhelmed with joy. I mean, there are no words to express the joy I felt that day. Today, I can attest to Craig's claim of driving in his sleep because I have witnessed his masterful driving from Illinois to Florida.

Before I proceed to the Sunshine State and commence writing the next chapter of my life in the USA, I have one last bone to pick at the residents of Illinois, the Land of Lincoln. I would like to know why I was not forewarned that your wonderful opportunities were also prepackaged with snow, sleet, ice, and many, many days of brutal, subzero-degree temperatures? I distinctly remember the only thing that the immigration officer said to me when I arrived at O'Hare International Airport on September 21, 1991, was, "Mr. Tomlinson, welcome to the United States of America. Good luck with your studies!" He clearly noticed that I did not have a winter jacket but did not say a word in such regard! Okay, I will give him the benefit of the doubt because he may have thought that I had my winter attire tucked away in my luggage. Never in my wildest dreams could I have ever imagined a colder place. The subzero degree temperatures were quite brutal.

Please forgive my whining because here is what I really want to say. Most importantly, I would like to express my sincere thanks and gratitude to the wonderful people of Illinois, especially my friends, professors, and coworkers at the College of DuPage. I would also like to extend the same as it relates to the many others with whom I was affiliated while pursuing my practical training at the different companies. I found everyone to be very kind and caring. The warmth of the people was what kept me going throughout those subzero-temperature days.

I would like to make one last admission before I close this chapter. The above statement of not being forewarned by the people of Illinois is not entirely true. Actually, many tourists who had visited Jamaica from colder regions, including Chicago, did forewarn me many times while I was working at the Donald Sangster International Airport in Montego Bay. On several occasions, visitors expressed to me how happy they were to be in Jamaica. I distinctly remember two visitors came up to me, and one of them said, "It is [expletive] freezing back home. You certainly would not want to be there right now, my friend." I did not have a clue what they were talking about, so I found it a bit odd to entertain such a conversation. However, as a gesture of courtesy, I said, "No problem, man! Welcome to Jamaica." Or if it were a departing tourist, then I would say, "I hope it warms up when you get back home."

With what I know now, I strongly believe that those visitors were warning me not to migrate to the Windy City of Chicago. Little did I know that the day would come when I would experience firsthand the subzero-degree temperatures (minus twenty-one degrees, to be precise) that those "poor" tourists were really trying to convey to me. I simply could not understand what they were whining about. I do believe that if all Jamaicans were able to experience at least a week or two of subzero-degree temperatures, then and only then would they understand two fundamental truths. First, they would, just as I did, understand and appreciate the fact that Jamaica is a wonderful and blessed island. Second, they would, just as I did, understand why many tourists chose Jamaica as their favorite

*Chapter 2*

get-away destination, especially those who were running away from the subzero temperatures of Chicago. Finally, I must confess with all my heart that there were days when I had so much fun, like a little child who simply could not get enough of the snow.

Oops, I should not have parked on Snow Everest!

Am I barking up the wrong tree? Okay, catch me if you can.

I really need to get in, but where's the door?

As you can see, it was not all that bad as I portrayed it to be. Okay, I think you have seen and heard enough of my "cold talk," so let's get on down to the Sunshine State.

CHAPTER 3

# THE TREACHEROUS JOURNEY

### Are We There Yet?

Craig and I wished our friends and coworkers one final goodbye before commencing our long journey to Florida. The minute we drove out of the Lucent Technologies parking lot, it started snowing. I was happy to know that I was finally on my way to a warm and sunny state. In addition to the tropical weather, I had heard that Florida provides a Jamaican-like "no problem man" feeling.

However, the joy of leaving the snow behind in Illinois soon proved to be the biggest misconception of the journey. The closer we got to Indiana, the more it snowed. There was plenty of snow on the ground, and it kept coming down. And to compound the problem, I had no idea where Craig was. There were times when visibility was almost zero. I could see several vehicles, including a state trooper car, that had run off the road and got stuck in the ditch. Although I was quite worried, I decided to keep going, while reminding myself that this was not the time for me to panic. To stay on the road, I used the tracks that

## Chapter 3

were left behind by a semitrailer that was directly in front of me. This maneuver kept me on the road, because there were times when I was unable to tell where the road began and where it ended.

Back in those days (BCP, before cell phone), neither Craig nor I had cell phones, which meant that we were unable to communicate with each other. And for some strange reason, Craig, who should have been leading the way, ended up trailing a fair distance behind. Now I was leading the way and had no clue where I was going except that I was following the semitrailer that was directly in front of me. The semitrailer exited the highway, but I had no idea what had happened, so I ended up exiting the highway too. Again, the Lord was watching over me because just as I exited the highway, Craig saw my blue Ford Taurus going down the off-ramp. He sped up, came after me, and managed to catch up with me before I went too far on the local road. He pulled up alongside my car and signaled to me to pull into the gas station that was located a few feet ahead of us. He came over to my car and asked, "Are you running low on fuel?" I told him that I had more than enough fuel and explained to him what had happened. It was so hilarious to the point that we both could not hold back the laughter.

Nonetheless, Craig said, "Seeing that we are here, we might as well fill up our tanks." Just before we entered the highway, Craig pulled up alongside my car and said, "Stay behind me, I am the one leading the way, remember!" With no hesitation whatsoever, I relinquished all leadership roles to Craig. After driving for another seventy miles in the brutal weather, Craig pulled off into a rest area. Craig was leading the way, which meant I had no choice but to follow along and take breaks only when he

## The Treacherous Journey

did. For our first stop, we took a break of approximately ten to fifteen minutes. After we were through with our break, I remember Craig took off in his shiny new Buick and left me far behind. It appeared as though my car were going backward or at a standstill. It took me a good while driving at a top speed of 85 mph before I finally caught up. Every time we entered the highway, I was playing catch up. Craig's new car had to be a V6 because I was never able to match his initial acceleration. My Ford Taurus had no concept of initial acceleration. It had a "soon come man" Jamaican mentality. I had never anticipated that the day would come when I needed to exceed the Ford Taurus' 85 mph speed limit. Well, I should not have such a negative view of the Ford Taurus because I had a whole carload of "bangarang" to haul with me to Florida.

Now that you have gotten a sneak peek of how the journey unfolded, let's get back to what happened after the first stop. After my first break, I was feeling great! I felt as though I could drive for another five thousand miles nonstop. However, that was just an illusion because, after enduring another one hundred miles' drive, I felt as though I had not taken a break since I had started the journey. My entire body was aching. I wish I had a cell phone so that I could have let Craig know that I needed more frequent stops. After another 150 miles of gruesome driving, Craig pulled off into a rest area. Finally, I was able to stretch my arms, legs, and back. I wanted to let Craig know that I had never driven so many miles before and would appreciate it if we could increase the frequency of the breaks. However, seeing that he was being kind enough to escort me to Florida, then the least I could do was to adhere to his leadership routine.

## Chapter 3

We spent approximately fifteen minutes, and then it was time to hit the road again. For the second time, I was feeling great! I felt as though I could keep on driving forever. Once again, that was just a figment of my imagination because, after another hundred-plus miles, I felt worse than I had before the previous stops. My legs and my lower back were aching severely. I also started feeling sleepy, due to the gruesome weather conditions. We had gone through flurries, snow, and heavy snow, and now we were going through hail, sleet, and freezing rain. My wiper blades were covered with large clumps of ice, thus making it impossible to clean the windshield. Throughout the journey, I kept playing an uplifting song in which the singer proclaimed, "The joy of the Lord is my strength."

After driving for a while, it was quite obvious that the daylight hours were pretty much over. I was a bit worried because I felt as if I were about to pass out behind the wheel. There were times throughout the journey when I found myself trailing at a good distance, with no clue where I was. To complicate the matter, I was not sure if Craig had realized that I was nowhere in sight. After driving for approximately nine and a half hours, I was just going with the wind. It was not the same for Craig because he was blazing through the night like an Indy racecar driver.

Everything was fine until I found out that Craig was nowhere in sight, and I was unable to catch up. I floored the accelerator of my Ford Taurus and began traveling at max speed. As I came over a slope at full speed, I saw several flashing lights but chose to ignore them and kept on "blazing" through the night. However, within a split second, I realized that the lights that I had ignored were indicating to me that there was some sort of emergency situation ahead. To compound the problem, the poor visibility impaired my vision to the point that I drove by a person who was signaling me to pull over. I only had a split second to react. I was not about to apply the brakes, so I had no other choice but to squeeze between the truck and the other vehicles that were either involved or assisting with the accident. I narrowly escaped hitting any of the vehicles or the people that were at the scene. Every time that I reflect on this incident, I know for sure that I was not the one who had performed that skillful maneuver. God had been in control of the wheel because I was coming at top speed, with poor visibility, and had little or no time to react.

By this time, Craig had seen the accident and had pulled off onto the shoulder, hoping that I would do the same. Lucky for me, Craig saw when I swooshed by like a daredevil. I was going at full speed off into the distance, not knowing if I had left Craig behind or if he were miles ahead. After seeing what had transpired, Craig had no choice but to get in his car and come after me.

After driving for a while at a very fast pace, he finally caught up with me and beckoned for me to pull over. I remember seeing this person instructing me to pull over, but I kept going because there was no streetlight, and I was not about to pull over for someone I did not know. Moreover, Craig was the last person I was expecting to see coming from behind. Anyway, after taking a closer look, I noticed that it was Craig. I slowed down, and Craig went in front and pulled off onto the shoulder, and I followed suit. Craig exited his car, hurried over to my car, and said, "Did you not see the accident back there?" Before I could answer, he said, "Okay, let's get off at the next exit and call

## Chapter 3

it a night." The minute I heard those words, I breathed a huge sigh of relief. I really needed to get from behind the wheel of that moving object. Craig had seen enough and was not about to take any chances. With that in mind, he ended the journey for the night. It was approximately 10:30 p.m., and we had been driving for over nine hours through some of the worst conditions imaginable.

Craig took the lead and, as promised, he made the first exit off the highway and stopped at the closest motel. Before we booked in, Craig suggested that if I wanted to save some money, he and I could share one room. Seeing that I was already some six thousand dollars in the red as it pertained to my college expenses, I graciously accepted his generous offer. Little did I realize that I had just made the biggest mistake of my life! Sharing a room with Craig turned out to be the worst cost-saving measure I had ever enacted. Keep reading, and you will concur that I am not embellishing.

After Craig was through with the booking process, we took our needed luggage and proceeded to the assigned room. I was too tired to take a shower, so I went to bed hoping to get a good night's sleep; or let me say, that was what I had thought. However, just as I dozed off, I was jolted out of my sleep by Craig's loud and jarring snores. I was hoping that it would only last for a short while but, unfortunately, that was merely wishful thinking. Craig snored all night long! Never in my entire life have I heard anyone snore as loudly as Craig did that night! The night was long, miserable, and painful for me. When it was all over, I was happy to see the dawn of a new day. Later that morning, Craig got up and, with a pleasant smile all over his face, asked, "Did you have a good night's sleep?" I

## The Treacherous Journey

replied with an enthusiastic, "Yes, I did," because I did not want to give him the impression that I was not grateful for his offer. Then he replied, "Me too," followed by an even bigger smile. Probably I should have let him know that he had snored all night long like an old, miserable, wild boar.

Anyway, we showered, packed our bags, and checked out of the motel. We went across the street where we had breakfast. I am not sure if it was at an IHOP or an LHOP. What I do remember is that Craig paid for my meal as well. After breakfast, we went to the gas station (petrol station if you are British), filled our tanks, cleaned our windshields, and finally continued our long journey to Florida. After approximately two hours of driving, I was feeling exhausted and sleepy. I was hoping that Craig would stop for a quick break but, instead, he kept pressing ahead. We drove for approximately 250 miles, then Craig pulled off the road into a rest area. By this time, I felt as though I were breathing my last breath. I had not slept in almost twenty-four hours, and the members of my body felt as though they were being ripped apart limb by limb. After approximately fifteen minutes' rest, we continued our journey for another two hundred-plus miles before taking another break. As for me, I felt like taking longer breaks, but I could not because Craig was leading the way, and he meant business. As you have realized by now, Craig was my human GPS. I was always happy when Craig turned on his indicator and pulled off into a rest area.

After our second break, Craig decided that he was going to cover a lot more miles before taking another break. With that said, he kept on passing one rest area after another. I was in my car, hoping and praying that he would stop, but he kept on going and going as if he

## Chapter 3

were the Energizer bunny. After driving endlessly for several hours, I finally saw the glowing Welcome to Florida sign. Ladies and gentlemen, at that moment, I was one of the happiest people alive! I immediately assumed that Ft Lauderdale was just a couple of miles away. Or in the words of a Jamaican, "Ft Lauderdale deh jus roun di cawna" (Ft Lauderdale is just around the corner). However, little did I realize that I had been fooled, bamboozled, and Houdinied by the big, bright, shiny, and deceptive "Welcome to Florida" sign. I had no idea that my journey had only just begun, and that we had hundreds of miles to go.

After seeing the Welcome to Florida sign, I kept looking out for the Coconut Creek exit. I kept a watchful eye on Craig's car, hoping to see his flashing indicator signaling that he was getting ready to exit the highway. Once again, I was just fooling myself because I had absolutely no knowledge regarding the geographical layout of Florida. Probably I should have done a bit of homework on the state of Florida but, instead, I had left everything up to Craig. After driving several hours and way too many miles, I finally saw Craig put his indicator on and pull off into a rest area. The minute we parked, I got out of my car, ran over to Craig's car, and asked, "Craig, are we in Florida?"

He smiled and said, "Yeah." Then he stared at me as if I had asked him one of those "gotcha" questions. I asked him how far away we were from Coconut Creek, and that was when he smiled again and said, "Get ready; we still have a long way to go." He then walked over to a map that was on the wall and showed me the geographical layout of Florida. Ladies and gentlemen, that was when I realized that we, indeed, had a long way and many more hours of driving to go. However, as it pertained to Florida, I still

## The Treacherous Journey

was unable to match my perception of reality; that is, how much driving time it would take to get to our destination.

After a short break, we went back on the highway and continued our never-ending journey. As time ticked away and Coconut Creek was nowhere in sight, I began to feel all sorts of aches and pains. The pain that was radiating in my lower back was excruciating. Every time that we approached a town, I was hoping and praying that we were at Coconut Creek. However, my hoping and praying dissipated rather quickly when I observed that Craig kept up his speed and just blew right through the town like a whirlwind. It was as if we were back on the vast open plains where not even the "Little House on the Prairie" existed. By this time, it was pitch dark, which was a lot more telling while we were going through the "noman's lands." Not only that, but since having entered Florida, I had yet to see any sunshine. I believe that it would have been more appropriate to refer to Florida as the Darknight State instead of the Sunshine State. By this time, I had become a zombie behind the wheel. I had no sense of reasoning. I just did not know what was really going on around me. After approximately twenty-four hours of driving, and not getting any sleep in almost thirty-two hours, I finally! saw Craig's indicator flashing, and his car started moving toward the right lane. That was when I breathed a loud sigh of relief, and all the pain and fatigue went away briefly.

After a few tight maneuvers, Craig and I exited the highway onto the local road. Within a couple of minutes, we finally made it to his mother's home. After finding a parking place, I got out of the car and did a complete "360" stretch of all my joints and muscles. After I was through stretching, Craig signaled to me to follow him.

## Chapter 3

We went inside the apartment, where he introduced me to his mother, Adele. After the short meet and greet, I sat on the couch to relax a bit. Sitting on the couch was the last thing I remember doing because I had an out-of-body experience. In addition to the pain, I had developed a high fever. This was one of those inferno-type fevers that caused me to feel like I was on fire. I do believe this is what Alicia Keys meant when she said, "This boy is on fire!" Or was it "This girl is on fire!" Regardless of the gender, the point is that I was roasting with fever. The lack of sleep had taken a toll on me. When I woke up some three hours later somewhere around 2:00 a.m., Craig said to me, "You were knocked out, and we just had to let you sleep." After a short conversation, I bid Craig one final goodbye before continuing with the next phase of my journey.

Before I proceed, I would like to express my sincere thanks and gratitude to Craig because he is indeed a "Goodman." Just to let you know, I added a little pun because Craig's surname is Goodman. Nonetheless, he is indeed more than a good man because I could not have asked for anything more of him.

I was now faced with the harsh reality of finding my friend's home, without the aid of a human GPS. Let's find out how the shortest leg of the journey unfolded. I did not have a map, which meant that I had to rely on the directions that Craig had given me, which did not go according to plan. So, after making several U-turns, I finally decided to stop at a gas station and ask for directions. After stopping at the first gas station, I was a bit surprised when I found out that the attendant did not speak a word of English. All he was able to say to me was, "No, hablo Inglés." At the time, I had no clue what he was saying. For a minute,

I thought I was at the Tower of Babel. This was my first visit to the Sunshine State, and I realized that I had a lot to learn, including Spanish.

I decided that, instead of stopping at another gas station, I would search for a public phone and contact my friend. After navigating around for a while, I finally found one that worked. I contacted Michael, but he was unable to tell me exactly where I was or how to get back to State Road 7. Nonetheless, he told me that 19th Street ran across State Road 7, and the apartment complex was located on the west side of the street.

After locating State Road 7 (441/SR 7) and after numerous U-turns, tight maneuvers, and eye-popping stares, I finally located 19th street. However, I was going way too fast, so I blew by 19th Street, went a little further north, and made one final U-turn. Heck, I had made so many U-turns, what was another one going to do, delay my journey? I made a right onto 19th Street, then drove a short distance to the housing complex. It wasn't until after I had exited the car and made one final 360-degree stretch that it dawned on me that the ordeal was finally over. It was the grace of God and Craig's outstanding leadership that had made it possible for me to reach my destination safely.

After that short flashback of my treacherous journey, I navigated through the building until I located Michael's apartment. The minute I knocked on the door, he opened it and invited me inside. After a short meet and greet with him and his wife, Prudence[4], he said, "My yout, I don't

---

4 As a reminder, Prudence was one of the HEART trainees who was awarded scholarship to study at the College of Dupage. She was also my roommate while living in Illinois.

## Chapter 3

think it's a good idea to leave the computers and the other valuable items inside the car overnight." In my mind, I was saying, "Yes! It is a good idea to leave them there," because unloading the car at approximately 3:30 a.m. in the morning was the last thing on my mind. However, with a little more convincing, I decided to heed his advice. In a way, I was happy that I did because I would have been highly upset if someone had stolen my expensive computers. After we were through, we called it a night and retired to bed. Well, we did everything except for the retire to bed part, because my friends had only one room in the apartment. So, while they retired to bed, I retired to the couch in the living room.

CHAPTER 4

# LIFE IN THE SUNSHINE STATE

After having spent the previous five winters in Chicago, I finally was in a place that reminded me of the tropical island of Jamaica. Well, it was not all cool runnings, because my first Sunshine State experience came in the form of severe pain. I woke up the next morning with pain radiating from every square inch of my body. The source of my pain was traced back to my roommates' couch, which was badly worn. I should not be complaining too much because the sofa became my resting place for approximately three more months. Anyway, here is how my new life in Florida began. Although I was fully accepted to the undergraduate program at Florida Atlantic University (FAU), I had one last hurdle to overcome. That is, I had to renew my student visa, which is the most important requirement for all international students.

**Back to the Island to Renew My Student Visa**

The first step in the process was for me to make another trip to the United States Embassy located in Kingston, Jamaica. Time was of the essence, so I went ahead and purchased

## Chapter 4

a round-trip ticket from Air Jamaica. The cheapest airfare was going for a whopping $450, and it surely placed another dent in my already limited funds.

After landing in Jamaica, for some unknown reason, I started to have second thoughts. On the one hand, I knew that I did not have sufficient funds to cover the full cost of my undergraduate program, but on the other hand, I knew that I had enough to justify taking the risk. Nonetheless, I decided to discuss my options with my mentor, Mr. Tyson. One thing I had learned over the years was that Mr. Tyson was, and still is, a strong believer in continuous education. Therefore, it would have taken a life-or-death situation for him to have advised me otherwise. With that said, Mr. Tyson and I went over several what-if scenarios. Even though we did not arrive at a conclusive outcome, in the end, Mr. Tyson said, "Tommy, you just have to give yourself a chance. So my advice is that you go ahead with your plan and see what happens."

Before I made my trip to the US Embassy, I visited my foster mother and presented her with the wonderful news of my accomplishment and how I was preparing to embark on yet another phase of my academic journey. I also let her know that as soon as I was through with my studies in the United States, I would return to Jamaica so that she and I could spend quality time together. I even went as far as to let her know that, upon my return, I would purchase a home in Montego Bay where both of us would live, that I would take the best care of her, and so on and so forth. After Aunt Lucy was through congratulating and wishing me success, she looked directly at me and said, "Desmond, I want you to listen to me carefully. I have lived my life already, and I want you to live yours, so don't worry about me. Do not plan your life around me, just put your hope and trust in the Lord, and things will work out." After hearing what my foster mother said, I immediately became despondent. I thought that she did not care about me anymore. I just could not make any sense of why she was not excited to know that I had included her in my future plans. I really wanted to show her in tangible ways that I was grateful for the overwhelming compassion that she had bestowed on me.

Nonetheless, Aunt Lucy encouraged me one last time, saying, "Desmond, just put your hope and trust in the Lord. Yuh hear mi man, just put your hope and trust in the Lord." Despite her comforting words, I was still feeling sad because I did not understand why Aunt Lucy was not too thrilled with my future plans. However, my failure to understand her rationale at the time reminded me of her wise phrase, "Boy does not know everything that man knows, but man knows everything that a boy knows because man was once a boy." I came to realize, some six years later, that every word Aunt Lucy spoke and every action she took was always in my best interest and not hers. First, Aunt Lucy was reminding me to let the Lord guide my future plans even if they took precedence over the one I had concerning her. Second, she wanted me to focus all my energy on my education and nothing else, not even her. In fact, she told me on several occasions that having a good education was the only way for me to make a difference in my life and the lives of others. I do understand that with or without education, everyone is capable of making a difference; however, in this context, Aunt Lucy was pragmatic because she did not want to provide me with false hope or blind optimism.

Chapter 4

My sisters, nieces, and nephews also encouraged me to move forward with my academic studies. They told me that I had a wonderful opportunity and that I should not give up on my dreams. On the one hand, I had learned over the years that not every action taken by a person will produce the desired or intended outcome. On the other hand, I am entirely convinced that God rewards those who work hard and have the will to persevere. I know that I have said this before, but I do believe it is worthwhile repeating, especially in this context. Accomplishing my academic goal meant a lot to me because I had witnessed firsthand the devastating effects that not having the desired level of education can have on a person. In fact, this is even more apparent because none of my siblings had the opportunity to attend college. Therefore, acquiring a college degree was something that I felt very passionate about.

The overwhelming support I received from my family and friends gave me the courage to proceed. With no further hesitation, on December 30, 1996, I went to the United States Embassy in Kingston and applied for a student visa. Without any delay, I was awarded a student visa.

**In Search of Higher Education**

On December 31, 1996, a bright and sunny Tuesday afternoon, after all the runaround and the vacillating were over, I boarded a flight at the Donald Sangster International Airport and was once again onward bound to the United States of America. Well, it was more like returning to the United States to continue with my never-ending knowledge quest. After completing a ninety-minute flight, I landed at the Miami International Airport.

Michael and Prudence told me that I could share the apartment with them to reduce my room and board costs. However, we needed a two-bedroom apartment, but the condition of the lease stipulated that my roommates had to stay in the apartment for another three months or pay a hefty penalty to break the contract. Paying the penalty to break the lease would not prove economical, which meant that we had to stay put for the duration. Not having a bed meant that I had to sleep on my friend's couch for the duration. Not only that, but it also taught me the true meaning of the "yes pain, yes gain" phrase.

I was relieved when we finally moved into a two-bedroom apartment, which allowed me to revert to my uninterrupted, all-night study sessions. The exciting results are listed on my first college scorecard.

```
F.A.U. SPRING TERM 1997 3J BCS       BA
CGS    3300    MGMT INFO SYSTEMS           A       3.0     3.0    12.0
COP    3402    COMPUTER SYS CONCEPTS       B+      3.0     3.0    10.5
MAN    3030    INTRO MGMT&ORGAN BEH        B       4.0     4.0    12.0
MAC    3233    METHODS OF CALCULUS         A       3.0     3.0    12.0

              CREDIT      CREDIT    CREDIT    GRADE
   TOTALS    ATTEMPTED    EARNED    FOR GPA   POINTS    GPA
   TERM       13.00       13.00     13.00     46.50     3.58
   FAU        13.00       13.00     13.00     46.50     3.58
   OVERALL   119.90      117.90    117.90    424.30     3.60
```

After the first semester, everything was going great! There I was, enjoying my "cool runnings," "no problem, man," festive island lifestyle. Oops, not so fast, here comes the old Murphy's Law. Yes, I am talking about the one that says, "What can go wrong, will go wrong." Or, as it was in my case, what can go wrong, was about to go wrong. It all started one day while I was at home studying with no

## Chapter 4

interruption. Oops! I think I spoke too soon because the phone is ringing, so let me find out who is calling. Oh, it's my roommate, Michael. This better be an important call because he knows quite well that I do not like to be disturbed when I am studying.

The minute I said hello, he said, "My yout, mi figet fi pay di rent. Look pon di table yuh si di check. Tek it to di office fi mi my yout." ("My friend, I forgot to pay the rent. Look on the table and you will see the check. Please drop it off at the rental office for me.") In other words, he was letting me know that the rent was due, and he would like for me to take the check to the rental office. Sure! "No problem, man!" Or, at least that was what I thought.

With that said, I took the check from the table, went directly to the leasing office, and handed it to the receptionist. She looked at the check and said, "This check is no good! It does not have a signature on it."

I replied, "Not a problem. I will just have to write you a new one on behalf of my friend."

She asked, "Are you living in the apartment too?" Not knowing what the terms of the lease were, I said, "Yes, I am!"

Then she said, "You guys are in violation of the lease because your friend should not be sub-leasing the apartment."

After hearing those words, I knew right away that I had just made a colossal blunder, and there was nothing I could do to change the outcome. In the words of a true Jamaican, "Blow wow! Mi inna whole heap a trouble now!" ("Wow! I am in lots of trouble now!") I am not sure how we ended up resolving the payment issue, but what I do know is that within a couple of days, the leasing office mailed my roommates a letter stating that they were in violation of the lease agreement. This was certainly a lot of monkey wrenches being thrown into my academic plan. However, instead of rectifying the problem, we decided to take the risk and disregard the letter because it was not financially feasible unless we stuck together. This was a risky proposition because if we were caught, we would run the risk of all of us being thrown out of the apartment. With that said, I took on the "hide and go seek" lifestyle. That is, I left early in the morning and came home late at night when the leasing office was closed. I did so until the situation diffused itself.

**The Passing of My Mother and My Close Call with Death**

That year, my troubles came in the form of a "one down, many more to go" domino effect. Shortly after the apartment incident, I received the news that my mother had passed away. The sad news got a lot worse when I found out that she had also been laid to rest. My sister had been unable to get in touch with me, which meant that I did not even get an opportunity to attend my mother's funeral or to bid her my final farewell. Although my mother and I had not had a close bond, nor had we established a mother-child relationship (as outlined in volume 2 of my autobiography), it was still a devastating loss for me. I had planned to go back to Jamaica after my academic career in the United States to spend more time with my mother but, unfortunately, that was no longer possible.

Shortly after the death of my mother, I was involved in a motor vehicle accident that added even more mental anguish to my already battered emotions. It happened one

## Chapter 4

night while I was making a left turn onto 19th Street. All I remember was when I saw a flash of light and heard a big crashing sound, followed by a jolting force that had me wobbling around inside the car. As we would say in Jamaica, "Dis yah a whole heap a bangarang." Not only was my life spared, but I also walked away from the accident without a single scratch. It was a miracle. God had spared my life. The driver of the other vehicle was also ok, except for a few scratches on his arms. However, his wife had to be transported to the hospital. My car was totaled. That was the end of my reliable 85 mph top speed, blue Ford Taurus.

Although it was a difficult decision I had to make, I contacted the other driver on more than one occasion to find out how his wife was doing. The first time I contacted him, I thought that he would yell and scream at me, and most likely forbid me to contact him again. To my surprise, he spoke with me at length in a fatherly manner. He also updated me on his wife's progress. Well, I should have expected nothing less because even at the scene of the accident, he had spoken with me in a very calm and caring manner. I remember his first words were, "Why are you young people always in a rush? Where do you have to be that you cannot wait?" What this elderly gentleman was saying was this: What is more important than waiting a few more minutes until it is safe enough to proceed? I can say without a doubt that the demeanor of this gentleman reminds me each and every day to be a lot more conscientious of my actions, especially when I get behind the wheel of a vehicle. However, the accident was certainly not the last of my emotional and psychological ordeals. With that in mind, please remain seated, because another phase of the roller-coaster ride is about to begin.

I was hoping that the living arrangement with my roommates would stay intact until I was through with my undergraduate studies. However, that was not the case because I had to leave shortly after the spring semester of 1998. My roommates had started a family and needed the additional room. This option posed a huge financial problem for me because I was not earning enough money to finance my own apartment. Neither did I have enough money to carry me through the 1999 fiscal school year. In fact, I was short two full semesters' tuition, including living expenses. With that said, I decided to move all my belongings into storage and then plot my next course of action from that point.

**The Boca Raton Thriller**

Before I continue with this thriller-like phase of my life's journey, I would like to take several steps down memory lane so that I can introduce a very significant person who changed my life forever. Throughout this journey, I will also take the opportunity to fill you in on a few drama-like episodes as well. These episodes will bring into context a very special person I am so eager to tell you about.

Michael and I used to attend classes at the FAU Davie satellite campus, which was located approximately twenty-nine miles from the main campus in Boca Raton, Florida. The Davie campus was much closer to home, which made it the ideal campus for us. However, not all of the classes were being offered at the Davie campus, which meant that we had to travel to the main campus to attend some classes. Therefore, for the fall semester of 1998, Michael went ahead and registered us for Principles Accounting 2, Introduction

## Chapter 4

Statistics (Stats), and Beginning Spanish (Finalmente! Yo hablo Español) at the main campus. However, there was a small hiccup to overcome. In this case, my accounting and statistics classes overlapped by thirty minutes. Why had I put myself in such a predicament? Well, this was a cost-saving measure because we did not want to spend two semesters driving approximately sixty miles to and from the Boca Raton campus. The drawback was that we had to forgo at least thirty minutes of the statistics class. This was a very difficult decision for me because I valued every minute of every class session. With that said, I was now in need of someone who would be kind enough to provide me with the first thirty minutes of the class notes.

Let's fast-forward to our first statistics class session. Now that all of the students (well over one hundred) were seated in the lecture hall, we were ready to commence our class session. Well, not quite. The classroom was filled with noisy students talking among themselves. As we were there chatting away, we saw an elderly gentleman, Dr. Slater, come in the hall and start teaching, but he did not ask the students to be quiet. I guess he had experienced this situation many times before and found that as soon as the students realized that they were missing out on important information, they would eventually stop talking and signal to the students beside them to be quiet as well.

Shortly after that, Dr. Slater got our attention by saying, "Here is a probability: Two people from this very class are going to become friends, fall in love, and get married." Ladies and gentlemen, that was when the entire class cracked up laughing. I even overheard several students responding with smart comments such as "Yeah, right!" and "Go on and teach the class with your bad self."

## Life in the Sunshine State

A Jamaican who was sitting across from me said something to the effect of, "A wah rang wid dissa ole man yah sah?" ("What is wrong with this old man here?") Nobody, including Johanna (I will put her in context shortly) and I believed that this prediction was probable. Okay, a little too much statistics, but the point I am making is that Dr. Slater's interesting comment really got our attention. After the drama was over, the class quieted down, and Dr. Slater continued with the lecture.

After we were through with the lecture portion of the class, we went to the stat-lab (statistics lab) to complete our introductory lab session and to pick up a copy of the software program. I remember I went inside the room and sat in the second row from the front of the class. The minute I turned my head, I saw a girl (she was very petite) sitting off to my right. She was so tiny that I thought she was participating in the "bring your little sister to college" program. Not really, there was no such program at FAU. Anyway, I found myself contemplating if I should ask her for a copy of the upcoming class notes. It was not an easy decision for me because I did not want to be a bother to anyone in such regard. I simply could not muster up enough courage to ask her.

Immediately after we were through with the lab session, the little girl who had been sitting off to my right came over and said something to the effect, "Hello, are you Jamaican?" To which I replied, "Yes." Then she said "I am from Jamaica too."

Then she asked, "Are you good with computers?" Once again, I replied, "Yes." Then I followed up by saying, "Computer information systems is my major." I'm not sure why I had to add the frills; probably I really wanted to trade computer skills for class notes.

## Chapter 4

In any case, she followed up by asking, "Could I get your number so that if I have a problem installing the software on my computer, I could give you a call?" To which I responded with a resounding, "Not a problem," and we exchange names and phone numbers. We continued our meet and greet exchange for a short while then we bid each other goodbye and that was where our conversation ended.

See how easy that was for her to come right out and asked for my number just in case she needed help. Why couldn't I have done the same and asked her to provide me with a copy of the upcoming class notes? I had let this opportunity slip away, which meant that I was still in need of someone to provide me with at least the first thirty minutes of the class lecture.

For our second lab, I found myself sitting across from the same little Jamaican girl once more. I know you might be asking why was I so fascinated by this girl when there were many other girls in the class with greater body mass. Well, I must 'fess up by letting you know that being a "small boy" myself, I was a bit intimidated by the bigger girls, especially the ones who appeared as though they could dunk a basketball right over my head. Nonetheless, it was a lack of courage that was preventing me from asking Johanna (a tiny girl) if she could provide me with a copy of the upcoming class notes. As I was sitting there contemplating, precious time was ticking away.

Knowing how important this information was, I got up, went over to her desk, and said, "Hello." She replied likewise. Then I asked, "If it is not a problem, could you please make a copy of the lecture notes for me?" She replied, "Sure!" Oops, I forgot to let her know that I only needed the first thirty minutes. With that in mind, I went back to her desk and said, "Hello, I only need the first thirty minutes of the lecture." She sort of knit her brow and said, "Okay." I guess she must have been wondering why I only needed the first thirty minutes of the lecture notes. Not only that, but she probably was asking herself who takes notes in thirty-minute increments. Anyway, that was where our conversation ended.

The following week, just as I was walking along the balcony that connected the lecture hall and the main building that hosted the statistics lab, I saw Johanna who I had asked to provide me with a copy of her notes walking ahead of me. I really needed to get her attention, so I started walking briskly, hoping to catch up to her before she exited the building. I am not sure if she had stopped or if I had caught up with her, however, regardless of how it happened, we ran into each other at the end of the balcony. She said, "Hi," to which I replied with a pleasant "Hello." Then she handed me a copy of the previous week's lecture notes. I thanked her, and she responded with a "not a problem" gesture.

After we were through with the lab assignments, and just before I walked out the door, she asked, "Can I give you a call, because I need some help installing the lab program on my computer?"

I responded with a resounding, "Not a problem!" I was more than happy to assist her, especially knowing that she had gone out of her way to provide me with a copy of the lecture notes. After our short conversation, we bid each other goodbye.

Immediately after that, I went to the library so that I could spend some time rewriting the notes that Johanna had given me. To my surprise, the notes had 100-percent clarity,

## Chapter 4

legibility, and accuracy. Not only that, but the notes were well organized. And to top it off, she had highlighted the main points. Okay, I can't hold out any longer, so I might as well let you in on a little secret right here and now. Johanna told me long after we became good friends that she had a little crush on me, and she would go out of her way to rewrite the notes so that they were accurate and would show off her best penmanship. Or should I say, "penwomanship." In hindsight, I probably should have told her that she was only allowed to take notes, not to take notice. Oops, I think I am going to pay dearly for this smart comment.

Well, I should not be playing Mr. Wise Guy when the joke was really on me. When Johanna's friends found out that we were dating, they were a bit surprised and asked her if she were really going out with that nerd guy who came to school dressed in a church shirt and a pair of jeans. Wow! Little did I realize how much I was being admired by the ladies.

Moving on with the irresistible friendship episode. The following week everything was pretty much the same, except that this time, Johanna and I decided that we should complete the labs and the assignments while the information was still fresh in our minds. With that said, we spent the rest of the afternoon completing the labs and assignments. After we were through, we said goodbye, and that was pretty much it for that week.

After several weeks of mostly routine activities, we decided to study for the first major upcoming midterm exam. I am not sure what came over me, but being around Johanna gave me a different feeling, one that I simply could not understand, nor explain. The more I tried to resist this strange feeling, the stronger it came on. As for me, the real question was, what was really going on inside my mind, body, and soul? Why did I feel as though my emotions were being caught up in an uncontrollable vortex? It was hard for me to rationalize what was really happening because I had studied with and had tutored several female classmates, and not once had I had to deal with such strange feelings. As a matter of fact, for the six years that I had been living in the United States, the closest that I had been to the opposite sex was a casual meet and greet handshake or a once in a blue moon, friendly hug if the other party prompted such action. I had simply been too busy soaking up knowledge.

Moreover, I had a schedule that mapped out every hour of the day, and I can assure you that relationships were certainly not included. To further prove my point, here is a real-world example. I remember while I was living in Chicago, my roommate, Ed, came home one weekend and happened to look at my schedule on the refrigerator and said, "You are kidding? This schedule is not real?" To which I replied, "Sure, it is!" Then he said, "I have never seen someone who manages his time to the point that taking a shower and talking to friends are accounted for."

Here is the rationale for such stringent time management. First, I had a hectic workload, and second, I am certainly not a speed learner. Therefore, it was important for me to resort to those stringent measures. I viewed sleep as a waste of time, especially knowing that sleep would eventually deprive me of valuable study time. I even went as far as to ask the Lord to remove sleep from me while I was studying in the United States. In hindsight, I am happy that the Lord overlooked my many silly requests, including that one.

## Chapter 4

I must admit that while living in Chicago, I tried on one occasion to deviate from my studies, but it ended up becoming a big distraction for me. Now that I mention it, I might as well put my current thought on hold and give you the full account of this drama. In the words of a Jamaican DJ, "Mi seh crowd a people, come hear dis!" One day while I was in one of my computer programming classes, I met a jovial but dedicated Vietnamese American student. His name was Seepo. I am not sure if I spelled his name correctly, but he will let me know the next time we cross paths. Anyway, he and I would spend many hours working on our programming assignments and projects. However, Seepo decided to break the consistent study routine by proposing a recreational, chill-out activity. He said, "Desmond, my wife and I are going out to dinner, but our roommate is also coming, so we are wondering if you would like to join us?" He also stated that this would allow me to get away from the books and refresh my mind a little. I hesitated for a couple seconds, but then I said, "Okay, why not." He gave me the directions to his home and the time to meet him there.

I found myself rethinking if this going-out proposition would distract me from my studies. At one point, I thought about letting Seepo know that I had changed my mind. However, for some unknown reason, I decided to give it a try. Later that evening, we went to a restaurant where we had a wonderful time eating and indulging in a little friendly chitchat. I remember saying to myself, "Maybe this going-out thing is not that bad after all." In other words, I found it to be a refreshing change from the constant studying.

Later throughout the term, Seepo made another proposition. He said, "Desmond, if you want to take a break from your studies, you can contact my roommate Beverly, and you guys can go somewhere."

"Like where?" I asked.

He said, "There is a club in Yorktown; it's a good place to hang out."

I replied, "Okay, not a problem." However, in the back of my mind, I was thinking that this going-out routine might cause me to deviate from my normal study pattern. Moreover, I was not accustomed to going out and had no idea what the heck to do. Probably I should have asked Seepo for a couple of going-out pointers before embarking on this unknown adventure. Where was eHarmony when I needed a little advice?

After much consideration and deliberation, one day I decided to take a break from my "all study and no play" golden rule. With that said, I contacted Beverly and asked her if she would like to join me at the hangout spot Seepo had suggested. She replied, "Sure!" With that said, we arranged a date, and I told her that I would come by and pick her up. The day finally came, and for some unknown reason, I became quite nervous. Not only that, but something in the back of my mind was telling me that this routine would become a big distraction for me. Regardless of the indecisiveness that overshadowed my mind, I drove to Beverly's home and picked her up. Not knowing what was going on inside my head, Beverly made the biggest mistake of her life by letting me drive. She was providing me with the turn-by-turn directions because I had no idea where I was going. In addition to not having a clue where I was

## Chapter 4

going, my mind was very much preoccupied with the negative impacts this going-out could have on my studies.

I remember we drove up to a major intersection with big red stop lights beaming directly at us. As soon as Beverly told me to make a left turn, I hit the accelerator and was on my way through the intersection like a crazy Jamaican "jiva." However, that was when I heard Beverly screaming from the passenger side, "Stop! STOP!" I slammed on the brake and managed to stop the car in the nick of time. Then she yelled, "What are you doing! Are you trying to get us killed!" And that was when I realized that my body and my mind were in two different places. My mind was at home while my body was in the car, "jiving."

After that embarrassing near-death experience, I was able to gather myself and drove the rest of the journey safely. The minute we went inside the club, Beverly said, "Let's go over to the bar and get something to drink." I guess that with what had just transpired, she really needed a drink or two to calm her nerves. However, it was quite obvious that the bar was the last place I should be going after performing such erratic driving. Moreover, that particular night was definitely not the night I wanted to consume any form of alcohol. No, sir! Not after remembering what had happened to me while I was living at the orphanage (for details, see volume 1).

Nonetheless, I accompanied her to the bar. She ordered a type of alcoholic beverage, and I ordered a plain, alcohol-free, gluten-free, pineapple juice. Okay, please ignore the gluten-free remark. For the entire time we were sitting at the bar, I found myself caught up in one of those déjà vu moments. My body was there, but my mind was not. After sitting there for a while, Beverly probably got bored and asked me if I wanted to dance. I said, sure. I really wanted to say, "I need to go," but I chose not to because I did not want to ruin her evening any more than I already had. With that in mind, I went to the dance floor, but my feet felt as though they were glued to the floor. I was unable to coordinate any moves, not even the first step of the famous "Electric Slide." After dancing—oops, let me rephrase—after wobbling around on the dance floor like a rudimentary robot, Beverly must have noticed that my mind was somewhere else because she stopped abruptly and said, "Let's go." I was so happy to hear her utter those words.

On our way home, Beverly did not like the way I was "jiving," so she asked, "Do you want me to drive?" With no hesitation whatsoever, I said, "Yes." I pulled over, and she took over the driving from there. This was a good idea because we both wanted to live to see another tomorrow. She dropped herself off and we bid each other goodbye. From that point forward, I went back to my "all work and no play" routine. However, before I end this segment, I would like to tip my hat to Beverly and wag my finger at Seepo for proposing this "taking a break" from your studies idea. Just kidding, Seepo.

It was certainly a lengthy and dramatic story, but the point is that, before meeting Johanna, I had one, and only one, thing on my mind, and that was my academic studies. So, let's get back to the events that led up to the point when Johanna became an important person in my life and the events that have transformed my life from Mr. Have-it-all-together to Mr. Confucius.

For several weeks, I struggled with an overwhelming emotional feeling that consumed my mind. The more I tried

## Chapter 4

to understand what was going on with my life, the more confused I became. Not only that, but this unexplainable feeling started to have a negative impact on my studies as well. This emotional battle was being waged on several fronts. I was not accustomed to having my mind preoccupied with things not related to my studies. However, I believe that destiny had placed Johanna and me together because no matter how hard I tried to brush the feeling aside, the stronger it got. This feeling had consumed me to the point that I was unable to focus on my schoolwork.

It was time for my first big statistics exam. I showed up to the exam with zero confidence that I would be successful. I remember sitting in the examination room and everything on the paper looked foreign. Things I had once known and practiced many times over, looked like gibberish. There I was, flipping through the exam pages hoping to find a couple of questions that I could answer. By this time, everyone started leaving the room, and the noise reverberating from the students pulling and pushing the chairs only made matters worse. This went on for a while until I was the only person left sitting in the room. After the time had expired, I became even more confused because I knew right away that I had failed the exam. As I lay in my bed that night, I remember saying to myself, the only way for me to get out of this predicament was to go back to the formula that had worked for me all these years. That is, I needed to concentrate on my academic work and nothing else.

The following week the exam results were posted, and as far as I could recall, my score was a dismal 56 percent, which represented an utter failure. I would have been much smarter had I stayed at a Holiday Inn Express the

# Life in the Sunshine State

night before the exam. Okay, before you go off scratching your head, just google Holiday Inn advertisements. I was devastated because I realized that I would have to get a perfect score on the final exam to receive a passing grade for the course. Just as I was walking along the corridor, I saw Johanna coming toward me from the opposite direction. I wanted to melt away through the floor, but that was only a figment of my imagination.

The minute we were within talking distance from each other, she said, "Hi, Desmond!" To which I replied, "Hi," but in a very somber voice. The conversation did not end there because she followed up by asking, "How did you do on the exam?

Once again, in a somber voice, I told her that I had not received a passing grade. She was very much surprised to hear that. However, what was even more surprising was when I told her my score.

"What happened! she asked. "Most of the test questions were similar to the ones we reviewed on the labs and take-home assignments."

That was easy for her to say, but as for me, the test questions appeared as though they had come from another planet. She was a little hesitant to let me know that she had received a passing grade. Anyway, she quickly changed the subject, and we talked for a short while, then I told her that I had to go.

The downward spiral did not stop there because that same week, I also found out that I failed my accounting exam. This was very unusual, and even my roommate Michael and one of my friends, Paul, knew that something was wrong. Michael asked, "Bwoy, a wah rang wid yuh bwoy?" ("Boy, what is wrong with you?") More like, is something going on in your life that is distracting you from your schoolwork?

**Okay, Let's Get It Together**

After the dismal midterm results, I convinced myself that I would do whatever was necessary to bounce back on the upcoming exams. At one point, I even thought about letting Johanna know that for me to be successful academically, I needed to work alone and spend more solo-time on my schoolwork. However, every time that I would see her, that deep-down feeling I had concerning her would not allow me to express myself in such a manner. So instead of telling her exactly what was on my mind, I decided to try a new approach. Instead of waiting around to say hi and to collect the notes from her, I would sneak out of the room the minute the class session ended to give her the impression that I had not been present. In other words, I would deploy the LIFO method. That is, for each class period, I would be the last one in (thirty minutes late as usual) and the very first one out the door the minute class was dismissed. Instead of using the lab that was designated for the statistics students, I decided to use the general-purpose computer lab located in another building far, far away. I was exerting all this effort just to avoid running into Johanna.

However, this hide and seek did not last long because I found out that I could run, but I simply could not hide. Johanna would inquire of me whenever she did not see me at the end of each class session. One morning while I was at my undisclosed location (the hideaway computer lab), I saw my roommate coming toward me. He said, "Bwoy, a yasso yuh a hide? Yuh girl a look fi yuh my youth." ("Boy, this is where you are hiding? Your girlfriend is looking for you.") At first, I did not believe Michael because, from my perspective, it was highly unlikely that Johanna would come all the way to the Fleming Hall building just to give me the lecture notes. However, I was wrong because, within a couple seconds, I saw Johanna coming toward me.

Oops, I was outed. My friend had blown my covert operation. I should have a special prosecutor look into this case. Well, he was not at fault because he had no idea that I was hiding from Johanna. Anyway, Johanna gave me the notes for the current and previous class sessions and asked if I would like to study later. I thanked her for the notes and affirmed that it was ok for us to study later. After thinking things over, I convinced myself that probably I was the one making a big deal out of nothing, and all I needed to do was to relax and concentrate on my studies. Not only that but if Johanna could be successful in her studies, then so could I.

As time went by, Johanna introduced me to her mother and her brother. I even attended a couple of her brother's soccer matches. However, our first real social event came when she invited me to a friend's birthday party on the Palm Beach Princess. The Palm Beach Princess was a casino, food, and entertainment boat located in West Palm Beach, Florida. We were not there for any of the casino activities but simply for the food and the entertainment. Well, I should have tried my luck with the slot machines because from an academic viewpoint, I was losing big time! At first I wanted to say no, but once again, I said to myself, what could one Friday evening on a boat do to my studies? It was not like I was going "overboard" with this going-out thing. Anyway,

Chapter 4

we enjoyed the buffet, and then we went to the upper deck and enjoyed an evening of fun-filled musical entertainment. Later that evening, I presented her with a little token of appreciation (a gold chain; nothing too expensive, of course) for her overwhelming kindness, especially for the well-written class notes. Finally, we took some photographs, and that pretty much concluded the evening's events. Okay, when taking into account how I had messed up what should have been a perfectly good social event with Beverly, I do believe that I deserved five romantic stars for the way I had handled myself this time around.

Although the short break freed up my mind and let me step away from my academic workload, it was time for me to get down to some serious studying. Moreover, I was now faced with the prospect that I had to study many more hours than I usually did for my final exams. The semester went by rather quickly, and it was time to sit my final exams. However, for some unexplainable reason, it appeared as though everything was going into the irretrievable areas of my brain. The semester was coming to an end, and the probability of passing my final exams was quite bleak. I remember sitting down in the examination room trying to decipher the statistics exam questions, but everything on the paper looked foreign. This outcome was a repeat of my midterm experience. Once again, I was the very last person to leave the examination room. I was spared the embarrassment of a failure because the quizzes and lab assignments had boosted my overall score. In the end, I managed to squeak out a passing grade of C+ for the course.

As for my accounting final exam, I was also at a loss. I was suffering from an acute syndrome, one I would describe as a mental debacle. I remember the instructor came over to my desk and said, "Don't overthink the questions; they have been selected from the samples we went over in class and on the take-home assignments." Despite his reassurance, I still could not believe a word that he was saying because it appeared as though I were seeing the questions for the very first time. I mean, they were literally unrecognizable. Even Paul, who sat beside me in the exam, looked across and noticed that I seemed quite perplexed and dismayed. At one point, he turned to me and said, "Yow brethren, a di same ting dem, we duh inna class" ("Hello my friend, these are the very same problems we covered in class.") However, that did not make the situation any better because, once again, I was the last person to leave the room. And right then and there, I knew that I had not done well enough to receive a passing grade.

Instead of waiting around until the instructor published the grades to determine if I had been successful or not, I decided to be proactive and followed him to his office. While we were riding the elevator, I told him that I believed that I had not done well enough to score a passing grade. He tried to quell my anxiety by assuring me that I probably had done better than I thought, but that did not work. Even though we were riding the same elevator, it appeared as though I could see him ascending while I was descending. Nonetheless, I asked him to please look over my exam and let me know how I had done. After he was through grading my exam, he looked directly at me and, after a long pause, said, "You missed the passing grade by a couple of points." Instead of asking him by how many points, I asked what I could do to acquire a passing grade. And that was when he reminded me of the extra credit optional research project that he had assigned earlier in

## Chapter 4

the semester. Yes, I remembered it quite well. At the time, I had not taken him up on the offer because I did not deem it necessary, which was very unusual for me because I was always the first one to complete any and all extra credit assignments.

Now that I was in deep trouble, I told the instructor that I would like to opt in for the extra credit assignment. He looked at me and asked, "Are you serious?" He went on to say, "It is not possible for you to complete this assignment in two days!" I told him that I needed a passing grade, and this was my only option. He saw the desperation on my face and permitted me to proceed. He went over the requirements, and then he reminded me that I only had two days to complete the assignment.

This was the first time that I had undertaken a business-related research project of such complexity, especially to have it done in such a short period. However, with sleepless nights and sleepless days, I managed to get it done, and it turned out to be quite a learning experience for me. First, I had learned the hard way never to opt out of an extra credit assignment again. And second, by completing this assignment, I learned the sources and methods of how to research, extract, analyze, and compile corporations' financial data. In fact, this knowledge came in quite handy throughout my future business-related research projects. Also, I must give credit to a web-savvy gentleman (whose name I am unable to recall) who assisted me with the research aspect of the project. Without his help, it would almost be impossible for me to have compiled that much information in such a short period.

Please feel free to review, but not to emulate my lousy scorecard, as indicated below. Hmmm, for some unknown reason, a 2.67 GPA got me disqualified from the President's List.

```
F.A.U. FALL TERM 1997
SPN  1120   BEG SPN LANG & CULT 1*   P    0.0   4.0    0.0
ACG  2071   PRINCPLS OF ACCNTG 2     C    3.0   3.0    6.0
CDA  4503   DATA COMM ORG IMPACTS    A-   3.0   3.0   11.0
STA  2023   INTRO STATISTICS         C+   3.0   3.0    6.9

              CREDIT     CREDIT   CREDIT   GRADE
TOTALS      ATTEMPTED   EARNED   FOR GPA   POINTS    GPA
   TERM       13.00     13.00      9.00    24.00    2.67
   FAU        38.00     38.00     34.00   117.00    3.44
   OVERALL   144.90    142.90    138.90   494.80    3.56
```

Notwithstanding the unsatisfactory results, I was delighted to know that I had passed both classes. If you are curious as to why I did so well on my CDA class, the answer is that I had extensive knowledge in the subject matter courtesy of the College of DuPage's outstanding computer information systems and digital and microprocessor technology programs.

To my fellow college students out there, here is a bit of advice for you. First, please try your best to finish college before you get caught up in any committed relationships, especially if you are light-headed like me. And second, never opt out of an extra credit assignment, because anything is possible and you may find yourself scrambling for those extra points at the end of the semester. Take it from me because I am speaking from personal experience and have the academic scars as proof.

After that disastrous semester, I decided that I was going to heed the warning and apply the necessary corrective measures. The daunting task was how I would move forward after all the drama that had unfolded over the past semester? On the one hand, I had convinced myself that it was time to go back to the recipe that had worked for me all these years. On the other hand, I knew that, deep down within my soul, I had an unexplainable feeling concerning Johanna. This feeling had thrown me squarely off my focal point. I needed to find the courage to make a decision rather quickly. How quickly? Before the beginning of the next semester, which was just a couple of weeks away. I was faced with two possibilities: either to find a way to let Johanna know that I needed to spend all the time in the world on my schoolwork, or I would have to let her know exactly how I felt concerning her. With that said, I chose the latter. Why the latter? Well, I am not sure, but I do believe the other choice would only have prolonged the inevitable.

After several days of deliberation, much consideration, and consultation, I decided that I was going to express my true feelings to Johanna and ask her if she would consider our friendship to be more than just social friends. I had never attempted such a bold, emotional proposition before, and it was not something that was available in one of my textbooks. Neither was it something I could just wave the Google magic wand and find on the internet. Therefore, I needed to give it much thought. Before making any decision, I started by going over several possible scenarios. First, I considered the adverse effect this choice could have on my academic career. Second, this could negate the possibility of my returning to Jamaica to spend quality time with my family, especially Aunt Lucy. Not to mention the big plan I had regarding going back to Jamaica to computerize the entire airport, and to establish computer information systems training institutions across the island. I must admit that for the little knowledge I had acquired, I certainly had several exciting and ambitious dreams. Aside from all those wonderful dreams, the most important question was this: If Johanna and I decided to embark on a relationship journey, then how would it work? Would she come with me to Jamaica, or would I have to give up on my going-back-to-Jamaica dream and instead reside in the United States? With all those looming questions, I needed to sit down and think through all the possibilities, because if I should make this commitment with Johanna, then there would be absolutely no turning back.

After all that planning, it finally dawned on me how silly this whole situation would turn out to be if she weres already in a committed relationship. Although I had not seen another person in the picture, you never know, he could have been living somewhere in the middle of Alaska. To be really honest, I was hoping that after I posed the question to her, she would come right out and say, "Sorry, I am currently in a committed relationship." Then I could finally get over my unexplainable feelings and move on with my uninterrupted academic life.

Let's fast-forward to the day I decided to ask Johanna if she would consider us more than just friends. Instead of meeting her in person, I decided to use the phone. With that said, I dialed her number, and the minute she said hello, I came right out and said, "Are you currently in a relationship with anyone?"

She paused for a couple of seconds, then said, "You mean boyfriend-girlfriend relationship?"

I said, "Yes."

Then she said, "No."

Okay, that was not the answer I had been hoping for. I had been hoping that she would reply with a resounding, "Yes, I am," but that was not the case.

## Chapter 4

She followed up by saying, "Why do you ask?"

Instead of letting her know the main reason why I had asked, I replied, "Just asking." Okay, here is a bit of advice for all the women out there. Whenever a guy provides you with "just asking" as a follow up to your inquiry regarding a specific question he asked, please let him know that "just asking" is not a conclusive answer. Anyway, that was where our conversation ended.

Seeing that there was not a textbook written for my unique situation, I decided to turn to a good friend for some advice. I remember explaining to Rick what I was going through. Instead of going through a whole lecture, he said, "Desmond, don't be too hard on yourself. Learn to enjoy life a little. Life is not always about school and books." I had been hoping that Rick would say, "Desmond, your academic career should be the only thing on your mind at this time," but apparently, he did not. Once again, I decided to give in and phone Johanna.

With that said, I picked up the phone, dialed her number, and expressed my true feelings to her in a very romantic, loving, and thoughtful way. Well, the loving and thoughtful claim is simply not true. To be frank, even to this very day, I am not sure what I said or how I said it. Regardless of what I said and how it came across, it was understood because she asked, "Does this mean that you want us to become boyfriend and girlfriend?"

And I replied, "Yes."

"Okay, I will have to think about it first," she said.

I followed up by saying, "If you give me a chance, only time will prove to you the person I am, and you will never regret your decision." In hindsight, it sounded as though I had taken that phrase straight out of a Harvard Business Review article. No matter how you dissect it, it still would not have earned me a single romantic point. In fact, it sounded more like a business proposition. In the words of the American culture, that must have been the lamest pickup line ever. Our conversation concluded shortly after that.

I did not know what to expect at first. However, the very minute I heard Johanna say, "Let me take some time to think it over," I knew without a doubt that she would return with a yes answer. Therefore, I did not see the need to convince myself otherwise. After approximately three weeks of deliberation, she finally came back with a resounding yes verdict. I was not surprised in the least; I had known that the answer would be yes because destiny would not have let it be any other way. From that point, our relationship grew stronger. We went out a lot more frequently. Well, that is if going out on rare occasions is considered frequent in the dating world.

Wait a minute! Remember the very first day of my statistics class in which Dr. Slater got our attention by saying, "Two people from this very class are going to become friends, fall in love, and get married"? Well, it appeared as though Johanna and I were destined to turn this probability into a reality. Despite the relationship drama, I was determined not to find myself on the brink of failing another class again. With that said, I had to find a way to balance this new life with my schoolwork and my marathon study sessions. In fact, I did not have to do much balancing because the unexplainable feeling that had been consuming me went away for good. All I have is two words to describe this strange phenomenon: unbelievable and unexplainable.

As difficult as it was for me to understand this segment of my life, so was it for me to put into words. However, one of the lessons I learned from this saga is that one of my weaknesses is dealing with vague concepts regarding intangible characteristics such as love and emotions. That is, I do better when there is clarity, when there is a rational explanation for something happening. So once again, for the young people, especially for college students, if you are light-headed and are unable to focus on college while maintaining a relationship, then I would strongly advise that you make your academic goal your number-one priority. Oh, and before I forget, please remember to have a candid conversation with your parents, counselors, pastors, and mentors. Hopefully, they will be able to provide you with the best advice possible. Last but not least, remember to pray and ask the Lord for guidance throughout your decision-making process.

Although it was a long story, I believe it was one that needed to be told, because Johanna had become such an important person in my life. Now that the unknown aspects of my life were replaced with clarity, my college life was once again back on track.

**The Unexplainable Recovery**

Back to the point where I was suffering from the loss of my mother, my only means of transportation, and, finally, the comfort of my home sweet home. Just as I was recouping from the devastating news concerning the passing of my mother, I found myself in another unfortunate predicament. This time it was the total loss of my only means of transportation, which severely limited my mobility. With that said, I was in need of someone to assist me in getting around so that I could take care of the more important tasks. Once again, my worries were replaced with joy when Johanna came to my rescue and assisted me in every way possible. She was always there to lend a helping hand and much desired emotional support.

Despite the emotional roller coaster caused by the loss of my mother and my only means of transportation, I did bounce back from my worst academic semester, as indicated on my record below.

```
F.A.U. SPRING TERM 1998
CIS  4935   SEM INFO SYS ANAL&DES      B    3.0   3.0    9.0
ECO  3003   ECON PRIN-POLICIES         B    5.0   5.0   15.0
FIN  3403   PRINCIPLES OF FIN MGT      B    3.0   3.0    9.0
QMB  3600   QUANT METHDS IN ADMIN      A    3.0   3.0   12.0

              CREDIT    CREDIT    CREDIT    GRADE
   TOTALS    ATTEMPTED  EARNED    FOR GPA   POINTS    GPA
      TERM    14.00     14.00     14.00      45.00    3.21
      FAU     52.00     52.00     48.00     162.00    3.38
      OVERALL 158.90   156.90    152.90     539.80    3.53
```

## Life without a Home

It's time to pick up from the point where my friends started a family, and I had to leave my cozy dwelling. Just when I had begun to mend the physical and emotional pieces of my life, another major obstacle was thrown directly in my path. I was now faced with the daunting task of finding a place to live. After many unsuccessful attempts, I still was unable to find a place that would work with my budget. I had depleted my savings and was now in a financial bind. Even if I had the opportunity to stay with my friends, I would eventually run into the same financial predicament. My entire outlook had become even more challenging because I just did not have enough money to cover the final year of my college expenses. Despite my financial

## Chapter 4

woes, I convinced myself that dropping out of college was simply not an option.

After putting my belongings into a storage unit, I was left with the daunting task of finding a place to live. Instead of spending time on intricate details, I will provide you with a synopsis of how I survived throughout the times I was without a home. Luckily for me, Johanna's mom allowed me to borrow an old Subaru station wagon that had been sitting idle in the driveway. However, on several occasions, it would breakdown somewhere between point A and point B. In fact, most of the time, it would leave me stranded just after leaving point A. Although this Subaru created plenty of drama, I will share with you one of the more comical episodes that occurred the very first day I drove the Subaru and decided to test its highway worthiness.

As I navigated my way along the I-95 highway, everything was going great! Despite the excessive noise coming from the car, I found myself thinking about my classes and where I would stay for the interim. However, just when I started to enjoy the "cool runnings, no problem man," Florida breeze, a strange thing happened. The car started to decelerate. The more I pressed on the gas pedal, the more the car continued to slow down. Within a couple of minutes, the car went from 70 mph all the way down to 45 mph. My problem was compounded when I looked in my review mirror and noticed that a semitrailer was coming down on me like a bullet train. I was very close to the overpass, and was worried because I did not want to pull off onto the narrow shoulder. I was hoping and praying that I could at least make it over the bridge before the semitrailer pinned me against the barrier. However, just before I reach the exit, I heard a loud and scary horn echoing in my ears.

I looked into my rearview mirror, and the only thing that I could see was the semitrailer's grill. It appeared as though I were backing up into a large metal object. The driver was very upset, because he kept honking the truck horn. I do believe that the driver of the semitrailer was determined to push me off the bridge. At that very moment, I was ready to say goodbye to this world.

However, just as I was halfway over the bridge, I heard a loud supersonic boom. And just in case you are wondering, the answer is, no, my car had not broken the sound barrier. Something had exploded inside the car engine. At first, I thought I had been hit from behind by the semi, but I realized that was not the case. As a matter of fact, within a couple of seconds of hearing the sound, I saw a cloud of steam gushing out from beneath the hood of the old Subaru. Immediately after that, the stifling odor of antifreeze started pouring into the car! The only good thing that came from this incident was the fact that the driver of the semitrailer saw what had happened and backed off. I guess he had thought that I was slowing down because I really wanted to be a Jamaican jerk. After the frightening ordeal was over, I was able to breathe a sigh of relief. I managed to coast the rest of the way over the bridge, down the ramp, and finally onto the local road. I managed to keep the engine going until I was about a quarter of a mile from the corner of Lake Worth Road and Military Trail.

I quickly pulled into a parking lot, and the minute I opened the hood of the car, the evidence was as clear as daylight. The radiator hose had a big split. Although the incident appeared to be catastrophic, it did turn out to be a simple hose replacement job. Instead of just standing there, hoping for a good Samaritan to come and rescue

## Chapter 4

me, I decided to walk to the nearest auto supply store. This was certainly my lucky day because one was located within proximity! I hurried into the store and purchased the necessary parts, including two gallons of antifreeze. I returned to the car and, in less than an hour, I had the new hose hooked up and the radiator filled with antifreeze. Hmmm, now that I think about it, I am not sure why is it necessary to use antifreeze in your car while living in the Sunshine State. Well, with the looming threat of global warming, anything is possible. Finally, I continued my journey to school via the local road, Military Trail. Hallelujah! After turning a forty-minute trip into a three-hour ordeal, I finally made it to school smelling as though I had just taken a bath in antifreeze. After that frightening but dramatic experience, I learned that the old Subaru was definitely not highway worthy. In fact, I found out that whenever I exceeded 45 mph, the car would overheat.

When I finally made it to the college, I took my bags and hurried off to the information technology department, where I worked as a part-time student aid. The minute I walked through the door, Jared, one of my schoolmates and coworkers, turned to me and said, "Kong, where are you going with all those bags? You are not planning on living out of the office?" Just in case you are wondering, Kong is a pet name that Jared tagged me with.

With no hesitation whatsoever, I said, "Absolutely not! I am staying over at a friend's home after school." Liar, liar pants on fire. That was just a made-up story because I had no idea where I was going to spend the night. Or the next college term for that matter. At first, the thought of living out of the information technology (IT) work area never crossed my mind, but now that Jared had mentioned it, it was an idea worth exploring. My first class was astronomy, and I can assure you that I was physically in the classroom, but my mind was far away in some distant galaxy. Not really, it was more like the little voice in my head trying to convince me that it would not be a bad idea to "take up residence" inside the IT work area. This work area was located in a discrete section of the building, which made it the perfect hideout location. It was also fully lit, equipped with air-conditioning, and had several large desks that could be easily transformed into the world's most comfortable bed. All I needed was a blanket and a pillow.

That semester, I did not make life easy for myself, because I registered for classes at the main campus and at one of the university's satellite campuses. The satellite campus was located approximately forty miles from the main campus. Nonetheless, I had nothing to worry about because Chew, my classmate and friend, told me that I could carpool with him. Having all those bags, I was a bit surprised that Chew did not inquire if I needed a ride to class or to the airport. Not only that, but I was not sure if my antifreeze smell was suffocating him because he did not mention it either. Or could it be that he had a number of these antifreeze incidents and was quite familiar with the outcome? In fact, there were times throughout the journey when his car sounded like it was about to fall apart as it labored along the highway. Nonetheless, his car was far superior when compared to my old Subaru. Despite the weird noise coming from his car (which we completely ignored), we made it to our destination intact and on time.

After we were through with class at 10:00 p.m., Chew offered to drop me home. However, seeing that I had no

## Chapter 4

clue where I was going to stay, I told him that he could go on without me because I needed to catch up on my studies. Chew knew that I spent most of my time studying, but he was a bit concerned and insisted on taking me home. He did not want to leave me knowing that I did not have any alternative means of transportation. That was a very generous offer by Chew, but he had no idea that I was just making up excuses because I had no idea where I was going to spend the night. After failing to convince me otherwise, he said goodbye and left. Later that night, I contacted Johanna, and she came by and picked me up. We spent another hour driving around until we found a cheap motel. I was happy to be spending the night at a motel because I needed to rid myself of the overpowering antifreeze stench.

The following morning Johanna came by and provided me with a ride to school. By now you must be wondering what happened to the old Subaru car? No need to worry because it was sitting comfortably in the parking lot at the FAU Boca Raton main campus. After I was through with my classes, I went to the information technology building and completed my four-hour work shift. Later that night, when my fellow information technology coworkers had left, I used one of my bags as a pillow and went to bed on one of the spacious desks. However, just as I fell asleep, I was awakened by the sound of heavy footsteps coming down the hallway. It was the campus police, doing a routine inspection. Although I did not see the person, I was almost certain that it was the campus police because of the unique footsteps and the jingling of the keys.

With that in mind, I got up quickly and sat in the chair, pretending that I was working on a late-night project but needed a little nap to reenergized my brain. Just as I thought, the campus police opened the door, turned on the lights, and started checking the cubicles. However, after conducting a spot check of the cubicles closest to the exit, the campus police turned off the lights, exited the office, and locked the door. Most likely, he or she looked briefly in the first three or four cubicles and did not come across anything suspicious that would warrant a thorough search. Wow! My heart was pounding after experiencing such a close call! I did not have a clue what I would have said if the police had caught me camping out in the work area in the dark. That was the only close call I encountered that night. I had little to worry about regarding anyone seeing me from the outside because this section of the building did not have any windows.

The next morning, I woke up with pain radiating from all areas of my body, which was a clear indication that the big and spacious desks were certainly not as comfortable as I originally had thought. In fact, the desk turned out to be the world's most uncomfortable bed. However, I learned to ignore my body aches and discomfort because I was determined to press on with my academic goal. So I got up, dressed, doused myself with cologne, and attended all my classes as usual. After leaving my 10:00 p.m. Critical Thinking class, I went back to the information technology office because I had not yet figured out where I would be spending the night. God knows I needed all the critical thinking I could get because college life had become a daily survival undertaking.

The next morning, I went to the school gymnasium to see if I could sneak in and take a quick shower. However, my plan was thwarted because the gymnasium was

## Chapter 4

packed with athletes. I wanted to walk right in and take a shower, but there were too many athletes using the facility. So I doused myself with cologne and hurried off to my classes.

I could not wait for Friday to come because I was desperately in need of my small but crucial paycheck. However, after spending a couple more days camping out of the information technology building and my most trusted Subaru motor vehicle, I decided to shop around for a cheap motel. After an hour of searching and comparing hotel rates, I found the number for a motel, the Boca Inn, that was located approximately three miles from the college. I dialed the number and asked the reservationist for the going rate. I do not recall the exact dollar amount she quoted but, to my surprise, it was the most affordable rate I had gotten thus far. Although the rate was very reasonable when compared to the other hotels and motels in the area, it was still not financially feasible. With that in mind, I started to bargain with the reservationist over the phone. She told me that she was not in a position to negotiate the rate, but that I could proceed with the booking and then speak with the manager in the morning. Without any hesitation, I took my bags, and off I went to the Boca Inn. As soon as the booking process was completed, I hurried off to the room. The first thing I did was restore my hygiene by taking a long hot shower. I was unable to sleep most of the night because I was up going over many contingencies. However, after much lamenting, I decided that I might as well get some sleep because, bargain or no bargain, I would have to pay for at least one night.

The following morning, I went to the lobby and explained to the reservationist (an elderly man of Indian descent) that I was an international student who currently did not have a place to live, and I would appreciate it if he could assist me with a more reasonable accommodation just for a couple of days. To be frank, I was expecting to hear him say, "Sorry, I am unable to help you," but to my surprise, he showed me great kindness. Not only did he give me a break on the daily rate, but he also swapped out my room for one that had extra tables and additional lamps to facilitate studying. In addition to the affordable accommodation, the location turned out to be ideal because it was approximately three miles from the college and was located on the bus route. Therefore, I did not have to worry about not having a reliable means of transportation. This great deal turned things around and gave me the hope I needed to live and learn another day. Whenever I was not in class or working my part-time job, I would go by the motel pool and study for a couple hours. After a while, this accommodation started to feel more like a vacation rather than a choice borne out of desperation.

With this additional expense, I could no longer afford breakfast or lunch, but I was very fortunate to enjoy a complimentary cup of rich hot chocolate made available by the Boca Inn. For dinner, I would order a large bowl of vegetable soup from the Chinese restaurant that was located in the shopping plaza across the street from the motel. Throughout such times I had to rotate my living accommodation among the Boca Inn, the information technology office, and a motor vehicle. Well, it was more like reserving a room at the Boca Inn when I was badly in need of a shower. Last but not least, I would like to say a perpetual thank you to my mother-in-law for reaching out to me through the desperate times when I really needed a

## Chapter 4

place to stay for the interim. These arrangements constituted my college life for a while. Little did I realize how important my mother's survival skills would have become. (See volume 1 for full context.)

Before I proceed, I would like to share with you an event that took place around the time I was homeless. I remember one of my classmates converted the cab of his pickup truck into one of the most comfortable sleeping cabins I had ever seen. Not only was his makeshift accommodation looking quite comfortable, but it also had an air conditioning unit that was powered by a portable generator. Throughout the hot and humid nights, I know it was all "cool runnings" for him because I could see the condensation running down the windows. It was throughout those times that I was tempted to ask him if he had space for two in his convertible pickup truck. I am quite sure he saw me outside sweating away in my AC-less vehicle but refused to offer me a night's sleep in his comfy cabin. Those were the good old days when FAU used to cater to the "Village People." Today, the university has become so modernized, I don't think we would be allowed to camp out like that anymore. Anyway, just a little humor for the mind, body, and soul.

Despite the constant running around like a mad hatter, by the grace of God, I was successful throughout all my courses, as indicated by my semester results below. With this academic result, I found out that being homeless was not such a bad thing, after all. Not only that, but I have just substantiated a new theory which proves that productivity level does increase when comfort level decreases. Guess what? I was back on the Mr. President's List.

After many months of ups and downs, I was getting ready to register for the last and final semester of 1999. But

```
F.A.U. SPRING TERM 1999
BUL  4421   BUSINESS LAW 1           A    3.0    3.0    12.0
CIS  4935   CRITICAL THINKING        A    3.0    3.0    12.0
MAN  4600   INTERNATIONL BUSINESS    A    3.0    3.0    12.0
AST  2002   INTRO TO ASTRONOMY       A    3.0    3.0    12.0

              CREDIT    CREDIT   CREDIT   GRADE
  TOTALS    ATTEMPTED   EARNED   FOR GPA  POINTS    GPA
    TERM      12.00     12.00    12.00    48.00    4.00
    FAU       82.00     82.00    78.00   276.99    3.55
    OVERALL  188.90    186.90   182.90   654.79    3.58
DEANS LIST 04/30/99
PRESIDENTS LIST 04/30/99
```

wait! There was yet another major hurdle to overcome. Academically I was surviving, but financially, I was in deep trouble. I did not have a single dime to finance my final semester's tuition and book expenses. Aha! I had just taken a course in critical thinking, so I had what it took to analyze, strategize, and, hopefully, to mobilize. However, after juggling many options in my head, I simply could not come up with a way to cover my final semester expenses. Establishing a vegetable business in the United States was surely not an option, because it was not like Jamaica where I had adequate land. Therefore, I was left with two options. First, to put my academic career on hold indefinitely, or second, to contact Rick, my Chicago friend, and hope that he would be able to provide me with a loan. Not wanting to give up while I was so close to obtaining my degree, I decided to reach out to Rick in such regard. Although I had known Rick as a friend for many years, I was still a bit surprised when he came right out and said, "Desmond, I know this means a lot to you, and I am more than happy to help in any way I can." Immediately after our conversation, Rick provided me with a loan to cover my college expenses for the fall semester of 1999.

## Chapter 4

**Yet Another Reason to Celebrate**

At the end of the semester, I was jumping up and down for joy, knowing that I had finally completed the requirements to earn a bachelor of science degree. It was yet another significant accomplishment, which was a bit hard for me to comprehend. It was time for me to get ready to attend the graduation ceremony. Okay, so why was I thinking about graduation when I had no money to purchase the necessary graduation attire? Although the graduation ceremony would symbolize the victory lap of my accomplishment, it was the least of my concerns because I was too busy planning my "going back to Jamaica" trip.

Once again, I decided to contact Mr. Tyson, my Jamaican mentor, so that I could provide him with the good news regarding my academic accomplishment. After he was through congratulating me, he said, "So, Tommy, when is the graduation?" Instead of answering his question, I told him that I had decided to skip the graduation ceremony. He followed up by saying, "Tommy, you have invested so much time and money into this phase of your academic career, so why are you skipping the graduation?" I told him that I did not have the money to purchase the necessary graduation attire. Immediately, he replied, "Tommy, don't worry, I will send you the money." And sure enough, he provided me with enough money to cover the costs.

Not only was I able to participate in the graduation ceremony, but I was also awarded the cum laude candidate distinction. It was a real joy or, as we would say in Jamaica, an "irie" feeling for me to wear the golden tassel. Okay, I had to maintain my composure because I was being carried away with my jubilant celebration. Not only that, but

## Life in the Sunshine State

I needed to get back down to earth because I had a lot of earthly things to do. After the jubilation was over, I purchased a one-way airline ticket destined for the sunny island of Jamaica.

Going back to Jamaica was not an easy decision because it was not like the days when I was single and could move with minimal resistance and no real consequences. Now that Johanna was a part of my life, the real questions were: What was our long-term goal, and how would we maintain our relationship from a distance? It was quite clear that what should have been an easy going-home decision had become an emotional dilemma for me. Despite the uneasy feeling, I was reminded that complex issues such as this always have a better outcome when placed squarely in the hands of God. Moreover, Jamaica is quite close in proximity to Florida, so I am not sure why I was so overly anxious concerning my destiny. With that said, I went to bed and hoped for a good night's sleep.

I got up very early on the final day of my stay in the United States and reminisced about the most notable events that had unfolded in my life over the past eight years. First, I would never forget the many freezing days that I had endured in the Windy City of Chicago. Second, the friends, professors, and coworkers I had met while pursuing my academic career at the College of DuPage and Florida Atlantic University. Third, the different companies where I worked while completing my practical training. Fourth and final, Johanna, her mom, and her brother, who had made me a part of their lives. However, despite the hardships, or those young mangoes from my dream, I can say without a shred of doubt that those eight years I had spent in the United States of America (1991-1999)

## Chapter 4

were undoubtedly one of the most transformative experiences I ever had. What started out merely as a dream in 1984, had become a reality seven years later. This dream had surely taken me on a journey that had ended triumphantly! Throughout such times, God had put together all the pieces of the puzzle starting from the very first day when it was revealed unto me in a dream.

Later that morning, I boarded an Air Jamaica flight and commenced the final leg of my journey back to Jamaica. As I sat there on the airplane, for a second time, I started thinking about how this journey had begun and how it seemed like just yesterday that I had landed in Chicago. Anyway, I did not have much time to think because, after a ninety-minute flight, the airplane landed at the Donald Sangster International Airport in Montego Bay.

# CHAPTER 5

# JAMAICA BOUND AFTER EIGHT YEARS OF KNOWLEDGE QUEST

After I cleared immigration and customs, I stopped by the main electrical sub-station to visit my coworkers. After we were through with our welcome-home, meet-and-greet celebration, I went to my sister's home in West Green. Upon arrival, my sister greeted me with open arms. Although I had not brought back any expensive gifts such as gold, frankincense, or myrrh, that did not stop her from extending unto me her warm welcome. In fact, she assured me that I was always welcome at her home. She was even more excited when I updated her on my academic achievements. As soon as I got a little rest, I hurried off to visit Aunt Lucy, who was delighted to see me. Her joy and her radiant smile came shining through when I presented her with an overview of my academic accomplishments. Although it was apparent that I had not brought back any tangible gifts with me, technically, I could still be classified as a wise man from the east. Relatively speaking, of course.

Chapter 5

## Do I Still Have a Job with the Airports Authority of Jamaica?

Monday morning, bright and early, I went back to the airport to discuss my return and to negotiate a position that would allow me to take advantage of my newly acquired skills. However, the human resource manager told me that the airport was undergoing privatization, and the Airports Authority would no longer be in charge of the daily operation of the airport. After several unsuccessful attempts to renew my employment with the Airports Authority, I had no other choice but to go job hunting elsewhere. I was very disappointed because I had been looking forward to giving back my time and resources as a way to express my appreciation to the Airports Authority for the support the organization had provided me.

Finding a job was not that easy. After receiving no job offers from the companies I contacted, I started to explore the next phase of my academic journey. I was in no financial standing to embark on such an ambitious academic journey, but I had everything to gain by merely exploring the possibilities. As the days went by, this academic ambition kept bubbling to the top of my mind, and I found myself contemplating the idea even more. At first, the master's degree program seemed like a crazy, far-fetched idea. However, the more I thought about it, the more I could hear a little voice inside my head reminding me that it was possible. With that in mind, I went ahead and discussed it with my mentor, Mr. Tyson. I remember Mr. Tyson looked directly at me and said, "Tommy, it is not going to be easy, but I think you should give it a try, and remember, if it does not work out, you can at least tell yourself that you tried."

## Jamaica Bound After Eight Years of Knowledge Quest

With that said, I boarded a flight and was once again on my way to the United States of America to explore the possibilities of pursuing a master's degree. A short, ninety-minute flight later, I landed at the Ft. Lauderdale International Airport, where Johanna met me and provided me with a ride to the Nova Southeastern University (NSU) main campus in Ft. Lauderdale. After discussing my academic and career outlook with one of the NSU business administration (MBA) program advisors, he was able to provide me with the rationale of why the MBA would be the best program that complements my information technology career. After he was through, I was convinced that this was the ideal program to advance my academic and professional career.

Moreover, completing a business degree at the graduate level had always been at the top of my agenda while pursuing my associate and baccalaureate studies. So, after a couple of weeks of comparison-shopping among several universities, I chose Nova Southeastern University.[5]

There I was, broke as a church mouse but defying all odds by embarking on my most ambitious academic journey to date. It seemed as though I had forgotten the mental, physical, and financial beating I had endured throughout the first two phases of my academic journey. Now that I had acquired all the necessary information, it was time for me to go ahead and apply to the Nova Southeastern University MBA program.

---

5 For a more in-depth look at the Nova Southeastern University MBA program, please visit *http://www.business.nova.edu*.

## Chapter 5

The first hurdle that I had to overcome was to obtain a financial sponsorship affidavit. Once again, Rick stepped in and filled this void. Without this sponsorship, it would not have been possible for me to acquire a student visa. After providing proof of financial sponsorship and meeting the academic requirements, I was finally accepted to the Nova Southeastern University MBA program. However, providing proof of financial sponsorship did not actually provide me with the necessary funds to meet my financial obligations, such as tuition, books, and other academic-related expenses. In fact, after calculating the costs down to the penny, I realized that my dream and reality were far apart. This "against all the odds" adventure did not come as a surprise because I had known that finance was an issue from the very start. Regardless, I decided to ignore the financial hurdles and push ahead with the next phase of my academic journey.

In life, there is always one last obstacle or "hanging chad" to get in the way of progress. Just as I was getting ready to commence the master's program, a representative from the International Student Affairs informed me that I needed to go back to Jamaica so that I could reenter under the F1 status. I had entered under the B1/B2 status, which meant that I needed to fly back to Jamaica and then back to the United States. There went my last dollar! With that said, on April 5, 2000, I boarded a flight back to the island of Jamaica. However, it was less of a hassle for me this time because I already had a valid F1 visa, so I did not need to go back to the US Embassy in Kingston.

Upon arrival, I decided that it would be a good idea to go and say goodbye to my foster mother one more time. I did just that and, once more, she was delighted to see me and to know that I was embarking on yet another phase of my academic journey. She gave me many, many words of encouragement. She said, "Desmond, I am unable to help you financially, but I want you to listen to me! You have nothing to worry about as long as you have the Lord on your side." At the time, a little bit of money would have been nice, but probably there would have been no need for all the wonderful encouragement if my foster mother had been able to finance my education. Anyway, she concluded by saying, "I want you to put your hope and trust in the Lord. You hear me, man? Just put your hope and trust in the Lord." Moreover, my personal experiences had taught me that money was no substitute for encouraging words, especially those that are considered lifelong motivators. With the overwhelming forces thrusting me forward, I decided to ignore the financial hurdles and push ahead with the next phase of my academic goal.

CHAPTER 6

# THE CONTINUOUS PURSUIT OF KNOWLEDGE

Now that all of the Jamaican requirements were met, it was time for me to begin the next phase of my academic journey. On April 6, 2000, I bid my family goodbye, boarded an Air Jamaica flight, and was, once again, onward bound for the United States of America. After a short, ninety-minute flight, the airplane landed at the Ft. Lauderdale International Airport. While I was on the airplane waiting for the passengers ahead of me to disembark, I took some time to think things over. However, the only voice I could hear was the one that kept asking me why was I embarking on this academic goal with absolutely no money. Anyway, money or no money, I needed to get off the airplane before it made a U-turn and I found myself back in Jamaica. With that in mind, I collected my belongings, disembarked, and proceeded to immigration and customs.

I presented the lady with my travel documents, and, with a Spanish accent, she said, "Mr. Tomlinson, what is the purpose of your travel today?"

I replied in a not-so-enthusiastic tone, "To attend college."

Then she asked, "Which school will you be attending, Mr. Tomlinson?"

Once again, I replied in a low-key manner, "Nova Southeastern University."

Then she said, "Congratulations, Mr. Tomlinson!" However, what really got my attention was when she looked directly at me and said, "By the way, Mr. Tomlinson, everything is going to be just fine."

I am not sure why she included that uplifting assurance, but two reasons come to mind. First, either, she had seen the doubt written all over my face and wanted to assure me that everything would be all right. Or she had just started her shift and was in a jolly good mood. Regardless of the reason, I looked at her, smiled, and replied with a pleasant "Thank You!" The way I felt, God knows I needed that little encouragement. After hearing those encouraging words, I took my belongings and went outside where Johanna greeted me with a radiant welcome-back smile.

My third trip to the United States was much different from the first two because this time, I was very fortunate to be greeted by a very special person. A person who cared deeply about my well-being. Johanna's mom and brother also welcomed me with open arms. Not only that, but seeing that Johanna was no longer living at home, her mom told me that I was more than welcome to occupy the extra room for the duration of my studies. So, as you can see, the good times kept getting better because I did not have to worry about where I was going to live. Neither did I need to camp out at the university, sleep out of a motor vehicle, or drive around looking for cheap motels. These wonderful opportunities made the transition back to college even more plausible.

## Life as a Graduate Student

I know you might be asking where I got the money to cover the expense for the first semester. Let me break the suspense by letting you know how I was able to pay for the first semester's tuition. One day while I was "out and about," I got a call from Michael Carroll (Mike), a good friend, and former coworker I had met while I was working at Lucent Technologies in Naperville, Illinois. He started out by letting me know that he had not heard from me for a while, and he was just checking up to see how I was doing. Throughout our conversation, I told him that I had been accepted to the MBA program at Nova Southeastern University. He congratulated me and wished me all the best throughout my academic studies. However, he did not stop there. He followed up by saying, "Give me your address so that I can send you something to help with your expenses." Wow! How did Mike know that I needed financial assistance? Well, no need to question or to underestimate the mysterious ways of God. A few days later, Mike sent me enough money to cover approximately 80 percent of the current semester's tuition cost. I can assure you that Mike's generous offer certainly exceeded my expectations. With that in mind, I would like to take this moment to say a big thank you to Michael Carroll for his sincere kindness and overwhelming generosity.

Finally, after all the prerequisites for the MBA program were met, I went ahead and registered for my first term at the Nova Southeastern University. My classes were scheduled for the weekends; that is, Friday evening from 6:00 p.m. to 10:00 p.m. and all day on Saturday from 8:00 a.m. to 5:00 p.m. The long-anticipated day had finally arrived and everything was in place, except for one minor problem. I had a one hundred-twenty-mile round trip to and from school but did not have any means of transportation. Once again, what I perceived as a problem was merely a matter of expressing my need to my future mother-in-law, which was exactly what I did. With no hesitation, she told me that I could use her vehicle on the weekends.

**The MBA Journey**

After approximately one hour and thirty minutes' drive, I finally arrived at the Nova Southeastern University campus for my first Friday afternoon session. I distinctly remember my very first 21st Century Management class that was taught by Dr. Gardiner. Dr. Gardiner was a very enthusiastic and entertaining instructor for sure. His philosophy was that learning should be taken seriously, but at the same time, learning should be a fun-filled event. However, as for me, I was trying very hard to contain myself because I just could not believe that I had commenced another phase of my academic journey. I kept on asking myself if what I was experiencing was real, or just a dream. However, after the first semester, I truly realized that it was real, as indicated by the proof below.

Term: Spring 2000
Academic Standing:

| Subject | Course | Level | Title | Grade | Credit Hours | Quality Points | R |
|---|---|---|---|---|---|---|---|
| GMP | 5012 | B1 | Twenty-One Century Mgmt | A | 3.000 | 12.00 | |
| GMP | 5015 | B1 | Law/Ethics | A | 3.000 | 12.00 | |

Term Totals (Masters - HCBE)

Other than advancing my academic career, what else happened in and around the new millennium? With all the hype and the overblown anticipation, the year 2000 came with a bang, but surprisingly, all was still intact. Wait! You mean we were not taken over by aliens or wiped out by the much-anticipated computer date glitch! Well, seeing that none of the overhyped expectations came to pass, then let's see what really happened. That year, Johanna completed all the requirements for her BS degree from Florida Atlantic University. She had chosen FAU with the hope of pursuing her master's in physical therapy, but had to transfer to the exercise science and wellness program because the university abandoned its physical therapy program. Despite the academic setback, she was able to complete the physical therapy assistant program at the Indian River State College (formerly Indian River Community College) shortly after that.

As for me, the year 2000 is one that I will always remember because, on March 19, 2000, I went ahead with my unforgettable marriage proposal. Johanna and I scheduled our wedding date for May 19, 2001. Okay, let's pause for a moment and take a walk down memory lane. Remember the very first day of my statistics class when Dr. Slater got our attention with his bold prediction? The one in which he claimed that two people from this very class would become friends, fall in love, and get married. Now that Johanna and I were one step closer, it seemed as though we were destined to fulfill Dr. Slater's probability. Please stick around for the final episode of this thriller.

After the engagement and the much-anticipated wedding date were established, I was once again moving at full speed through the MBA program. I was determined

## Chapter 6

to have it completed before my wedding date because it is a known fact that too much excitement does not go well with my academic studies. However, based on the MBA program schedule, I had to go beyond the May 2001 deadline. Nonetheless, we did not let anything stop us from proceeding with our scheduled wedding date. With that said, on May 19, 2001, Johanna and I moved forward with our planned marriage ceremony. Although my foster mother was too ill to travel, everything went well because my in-laws did a superb job. They did the cooking, baking, serving, decorating, and entertainment as well. Wow! These individuals were the Jacks and Jills of many trades. This was undoubtedly a significant cost saving for us. We just could not have asked for anything more.

Before I proceed, I must first remind you that you have just witnessed the final episode of Dr. Slater's probability, the one in which he claimed that two people from his statistic class were going to become friends, fall in love, and get married.

After the wedding excitement and anxiety had dissipated, it was time for me to get back to my MBA program. Finally, in August 2001, I completed all the requirements for the MBA program. Being an international student, and based on my inquiry, I found out that I was not qualified for any federal loans or grants. Therefore, I had ended up financing most of the MBA program with credit cards. I would like to emphasize that financing my academic career with credit cards was not a financially sound decision, due to the exorbitant interest rates. However, I did my best to minimize the impact by embarking on a few very skillful financial maneuvers. Have you heard the saying, "Robbing Peter to pay Paul"? In my case, it was merely borrowing from Mastercard to pay Visa and vice versa. That is, taking advantage of the zero transfer balance rates that were being offered for a limited time by one credit card to pay off a higher interest balance on the other. However, despite the minor financial hiccups, the decision to pursue the MBA program had been a worthwhile undertaking.

Before I proceed, here is a bit of advice for everyone, especially college students. If you find yourself in this situation or a similar financial predicament, please make sure that you are spending the credit card loans on things that are for the long-term and with significant value such as education or career development! Not on frivolous or superficial things!

Another opportunity cost that was associated with pursuing the MBA program was the many sleepless nights I had to endure. I used to lock myself in the NSU computer lab and study all night, only stopping for an occasional break. There were times when I was overwhelmed by the workload and felt as though I were about to pass out. However, throughout such times, I would place my textbook on a podium and stand for the next three to four hours reading out loud. Sometimes I would jot down the important points on the board while asking and answering questions out loud. Whenever I was too exhausted to continue, I would perform a 360-stretch of all my joints and muscles, followed by an exhaustive workout that consisted of ten to twelve pushups. If I could have found a way to speed up my brain processor, then I could have significantly reduced the number of hours I spent studying

Finally, I must express my gratitude to Aunt Lucy for her kind and encouraging words that kept me going, especially throughout the times when I felt overwhelmed. I

Chapter 6

must also express my gratitude to my wife for her enduring patience, especially in this regard. My mother-in-law, without a doubt, is and will always be the world's best mother-in-law. She stood by me every step of the way. I would also like to take this moment to thank my brother-in-law for his brotherly support as well. I would like to thank my friends and dedicated professors at Nova Southeastern University. Last but not least, thanks to my reliable Master and Visa cards for providing the funds that made it possible for me to accomplish another phase of my academic goal. With all these "Thank You," one might have thought that I had just won a golden globe award.

When it was all over, I was very happy to know that I had completed the MBA program successfully, as indicated on my scorecard below.

Completing this program is one more proof that with God, all things are possible as long as you have hope and the desire to keep working toward your goals.

Summer II 2001
Academic Standing:

| Subject | Course | Level | Title | Grade | Credit Hours | Quality Points | R |
|---------|--------|-------|-------|-------|--------------|----------------|---|
| GMP | 5102 | 81 | Leadership & Values Mgmt | P | 4.000 | 0.00 | |

Term Totals (Masters - SBE)

| | Attempt Hours | Passed Hours | Earned Hours | GPA Hours | Quality Points | GPA |
|---|---|---|---|---|---|---|
| Current Term: | 4.000 | 4.000 | 4.000 | 0.000 | 0.00 | 0.00 |
| Cumulative: | 43.000 | 43.000 | 43.000 | 39.000 | 152.40 | 3.90 |

Each time that I reflect on my accomplishments, I cannot help but wonder what it would have been like if my only brother had not been deprived of his childhood dreams. I could envision my brother graduating from Nova Southeastern University with his law degree and becoming a dedicated legal scholar. Why law? Well, I am not entirely sure. However, one thing I know is this: George was always challenging the status quo through his never-ending quest for justice.

CHAPTER 7

# DO I HAVE WHAT IT TAKES TO GET A "REAL" JOB?

Now that I had obtained a master's degree, it was time for me to go job hunting. But wait! I totally forgot that I needed to apply for permanent residency status before engaging in any full-time employment. With that said, I initiated the Immigration and Naturalization Services (INS) process that was required for me to obtain my permanent residency status. With not too much of a hassle, I obtained my residency status, or green card as it is commonly known to immigrants. With my vast and diverse academic knowledge, along with my environmentally friendly green card in hand, all I needed to do was to sit back and wait while a multitude of companies and corporations come crawling to me!

Well, my ego was deflated when I found out that I needed to do the hard work that is required to get a job. First, I sent out an unspecified number of résumés to many prominent companies. Second, I posted my résumé on several job-placement websites. The process was disrupted when, out of nowhere, came the September 11, 2001,

## Chapter 7

terrorist attack. It was a very horrific event that cast a dark cloud over everyone and everything. Throughout the turmoil, I continued with my job search, but the prospect of finding a job was becoming more difficult with each passing day. However, despite the bleak outlook, I was very fortunate to be working as a part-time student aid at Nova Southeastern University.

After sending out hundreds of résumés, I finally got the opportunity to attend several interviews. I would certainly not want to bore you with the details of my many rejections, but instead, I would like to provide you with a brief synopsis as it pertains to three of the more interesting ones. As for the first job interview, everything seemed to be going according to plan. However, the smooth sailing got derailed when the interviewer looked at my updated résumé and noticed that I had completed an MBA. I remember he said, "Oh no! I do not think you are the right fit for this job!" I followed up by asking why. And that was when he said, "You are simply going to use my company as a revolving door. As soon as I train you, you are going to become very attractive to other companies, and there is no way I will be able to keep you from leaving." Finally, he said, "My line of business is very competitive, and if you decide to leave, I can't just call up my clients and say, 'Sorry I just lost my developer, please give me time to find a replacement.'" I tried pleading my case but to no avail because he concluded the interview process abruptly. On my way out of the building, I remember stepping into the elevator, and the initial descent felt as though my whole life was going down much faster than the elevator was.

The second job interview I attended was at the Palm Beach Community College. After the interview, I thought I had the job locked away in the palm of my hands. Okay, as you can see, I simply could not resist the pun. A few days later, I got a call from the program coordinator, informing me that I did not have sufficient academic credits to be qualified for the teaching position. With that said, I found myself caught between two hard rocks. Academically, on the one hand, I was overqualified for the first job, while on the other hand, I was underqualified for the second job. As you can see, my job search had become a conundrum.

The third interview I attended was for an application programmer and structured query language (SQL) developer position. The interviewer was very pleased with my responses as they pertained to the application development aspect. However, he told me that he needed a person with strong SQL experience as well. I tried convincing him that I would spend my own time and resources to become proficient with the SQL language, but he would not accept my rationale. He reinforced his point by saying, "We are really looking for someone with at least five years of experience working as an SQL developer." That was where the interview ended, and once again, I was sent back to the unemployment queue.

I remember on several occasions while pursuing my MBA degree how a number of my professors distinctly had told me not to worry because, with my business administration and information technology background, I should have no problem finding a job. So much for those encouraging words. Nonetheless, the moral of the job-hunting story is this: If you are not successful on your first, second, third, or even your hundredth try, then just "keep on trying" because you will eventually succeed.

## Chapter 7

Okay, moving on. The interviews I outlined above made me realize that I needed to concentrate all my time and resources on gaining the practical experience that would allow me to hit the ground running. Not being able to acquire a full-time job with a software development company, I decided to accept a full-time position with Nova Southeastern University. Although my income was quite low (twenty-plus thousand per year) when compared to the overwhelming amount of school debt (mostly credit card) that needed to be repaid, I was very grateful for the job because it was enough to pay the minimum on the credit card bills. The interview outcomes had made me realize that I needed to be proactive and start acquiring the desired level of practical experience. First, I increased my debt substantially by purchasing a high-powered computer. Second, I acquired the latest evaluation copies of the Microsoft technologies and subscribed to online training courses and other open-source development tools and used them to gain much-needed knowledge.

Before I close this chapter, I would like to provide important advice to all job seekers, more so newly graduates. Please be proactive and develop your practical experience by applying for internships and other career advancement opportunities. Please do not wait for a company or a corporation to do for you what you can do for yourself. There are plenty of self-starter kits on the internet. Please take advantage of the vast online-training opportunities.

CHAPTER 8

# THE MIRACULOUS BIRTH OF LIFE

On November 12, 2002, at 11:45 p.m., to be precise, I witnessed the greatest miracle of all times. There is no other comparison because this one involved the birth of my daughter Julianne. This experience taught me that everything else is pale in comparison to the miraculous gift of life. A moment like this—to have witnessed the birth of my own child—gave me an out-of-body experience that is quite difficult for me to express in words. I would like to paraphrase a popular expression by saying, "Seeing is truly believing." Before this experience, I could only imagine.

There were times when I had tried really hard to bury the very thought of having a family of my own. I used to experience an overwhelming fear that the past would deny me the opportunity to express genuine love and affection to my family. On many occasions, I contemplated the idea of living a single life so that I would never have to worry about the intangibles (love and affection) that are associated with having a family. One of my most fearful concerns was how I could genuinely express love when my entire childhood had always been about survival? That is, instead of desiring to be loved and affectionately

## Chapter 8

cared for, my life was always about having someone or someplace to provide me with my basic needs, such as food, clothes, and shelter.

Moreover, if I had never heard a single "I love you" from my own parents or foster parents, then how could I pass on something that was never instilled in me. In fact, the only time I was told that I would be loved by someone other than God was when my brother and I were removed from the orphanage and placed in the care of our foster parents. And even then, we found out that it was a total fabrication. Instead, we found ourselves living in constant fear and humiliation. Not only that, but the most irreparable psychological damage was when our foster mother told us never to address her as a mom, mommy, or mummy because she was not our mother. She did everything possible to make sure that we did not become emotionally attached to her.

For all the years that I lived with my former foster parents, I had never received a single "I love you" from either of them. While living in Jamaica, I was not accustomed to hearing parents and children exchanging the "I love you" vow. After migrating to the United States, I was delighted to have heard and to have witnessed the opposite. I overheard parents, children, married couples, friends, and even strangers exchanging the "I love you" vow frequently. However, after living in the United States for a while, I began to wonder if the "I love you" phrase represented a solemn vow coming from the heart or just another ritual that was being evoked solely as a courtesy gesture. Concerning the above observation, I would hope that the "I love you" phrase is not a reflection of the latter.

This experience further explains why emotion, passion, and all the other characteristics of love are like abstracts to me.

However, I would like to emphasize that although Aunt Lucy did not repeat the "I love you" words aloud, it did not take long for me to realize that her compassionate actions spoke much louder and much clearer than the "I love you" spoken words. And that is why I truly believe that just to say "I love you" is merely a promise, but to exercise compassion requires a genuine call for action.

There were times I wished that love and emotions were as simple as following a recipe. However, today, I am very grateful that my wife is a very patient, understanding, and compassionate person. That is why I am convinced that we were destined to be together, and the unexplainable phenomenon that I experienced in the initial stage of the relationship was the necessary forces at work bringing us together. Although it was not apparent at first, as time progressed, my wife came to realize that I do love her although I do not repeat the words "I love you" as often as I should. However, despite my fears, the Lord let me understand that when certain forces are enacted, the results are far greater than spoken words.

Although it was not easy for me to understand or to put into perspective, today, I can say without a doubt that the birth of my daughter significantly diminished my lingering fears regarding having a family of my own. However, this does not mean that I understand how much love and affection a child needs, but what I do know is that I will keep on trying, while asking the Lord to guide me along the way. Last but not least, this is where fostering plays an important role in the life of a child.

## CHAPTER 9

# UNFORESEEN EVENTS

**Perpetual Knowledge Quest**

One of my greatest desires has always been to advance my academic and professional aspirations by learning something new each day. In other words, my life should have no idle time unless I am sleeping. The above aspiration is still my desire, but with a family, I am less rigid in my pursuit. Although I was quite busy improving my information technology skills, I was not being challenged by my job at Nova Southeastern University. Therefore, I needed to account for my time in a more meaningful way. With that in mind, I started looking around to see if other benefits or opportunities were being offered by the university that I could take advantage of. After a little probing here and there, I found out that the university offered tuition waivers for full-time employees. Although my timing was a bit premature, it was always my dream to use the final stage of my academic career to contribute to society in a meaningful way.

However, deciding what program to choose turned out to be a lot more challenging, because I did not have

## Chapter 9

the final phase of my academic journey planned out the way I had for my prior academic goals. Nevertheless, after searching diligently through the college catalog, I settled on the information systems doctoral program. Although it did not meet the significant societal contribution I was hoping to achieve, I chose this program because it complemented my business administration and information technology career. With that in mind, I decided to fast-forward my final academic journey and enrolled in the information technology program.

In 2003, I commenced the information systems program at the Nova Southeastern University (NSU). This was a bit more challenging than I had first anticipated. However, to succeed, I reinstated my rigid study routine by spending my nights locked away in the NSU Palm Beach Gardens satellite campus. At the end of the semester, my scorecard revealed the exciting result that I had been hoping for. It also provided the morale boost that propelled me forward.

**Term: Fall 2003**
**Academic Standing:**

| Subject | Course | Level | Title | Grade | Credit Hours | Quality Points | R |
|---------|--------|-------|-------|-------|--------------|----------------|---|
| DISS | 0740 | C3 | Telecom & Comp Networks | A | 3.000 | 12.00 | |
| DISS | 0840 | C3 | Prj/Telecom & Comp Netwk | A | 4.000 | 16.00 | |

**Term Totals (Doctorate - CCE)**

| | Attempt Hours | Passed Hours | Earned Hours | GPA Hours | Quality Points | GPA |
|---|---|---|---|---|---|---|
| **Current Term:** | 7.000 | 7.000 | 7.000 | 7.000 | 28.00 | 4.00 |
| **Cumulative:** | 7.000 | 7.000 | 7.000 | 7.000 | 28.00 | 4.00 |

Just as I was about to put my academic studies into overdrive, life presented me with several unforeseen events that totally disrupted my academic flow. The first unforeseen event was the fact that I was in need of a home. With the birth of my daughter, it was time for me to go house shopping because my mother-in-law's home was too small to accommodate a second family. However, I found out rather quickly that for me to be qualified for a mortgage, I needed a job that paid a whole lot more than my current salary. Having a master's degree that was mostly financed by credit cards and the desire to finance a home, made me realize that a gross annual income that was below thirty thousand dollars was less than a drop in the bucket.

Moreover, the interest rates on the credit cards started piling up. With that said, I applied for a position that was advertised by Adelphia Communications Corporation. After the first interview, I was offered a contract position, which I accepted. The news was even more special when the director of the Nova Southeastern University information technology division offered me the opportunity to continue working for the university in a part-time role on the weekends. However, by giving up the full-time position, I forfeited my benefits, which meant that I would now be responsible for my tuition cost. Well, that was not a problem because I was now qualified to apply for federal student loan, which I did.

## Off to Adelphia Communications

With much enthusiasm, I joined the Adelphia Communications workforce. I was very fortunate to have been assigned the liaison role between the company and one of its information technology providers. This job provided me the opportunity to ascertain a tremendous amount

## Chapter 9

of experience in the business intelligence sector. Okay, I should tone down my excitement because this is not the time or place for me to be updating my résumé.

In 2004, my wife enrolled in the physical therapist assistant program at Indian River State College (IRC). This decision did put a severe financial strain on the family budget. After looking at the bills, I discovered that math was no longer a guiding principle, because we were always in need of a miracle to just break even. At one point, I even tried to negotiate a salary increase, but Adelphia would neither budge nor budget. My manager was willing to consider my request, but she was limited in what she could do financially because the company was going through bankruptcy proceedings.

After working with Adelphia for approximately six months, it was time for me to research the possibility of buying a home. With my full-time and part-time jobs, I do believe that I should have qualified for a mortgage. Well, not quite. I found out the hard way after receiving one rejection after another. I had too many outstanding debts. Therefore, none of the financial institutions wanted to take a chance with me. However, all hope was not lost because my mother-in-law stepped in and introduced me to her realtor, Janice. Without any further delay, I contacted Janice and asked her to assist me with finding a home. The following weekend she took us home shopping in Port St. Lucie.

Why Port St. Lucie? Probably it reminded me of my foster mother, Aunt Lucy. Well, that was the first association that came to mind, but it was not really the deciding factor. The answer is that my wife had enrolled in the physical therapist assistant program at IRC in Fort Pierce, which was only fifteen to twenty minutes' drive from Port St. Lucie. This was a lot closer when compared to the roughly two-hour roundtrip commute from West Palm Beach. With that said, we decided that Port St. Lucie was a good place to start our home shopping. Moreover, the homes were better priced when compared to similar homes in the West Palm Beach area.

After visiting several homes, we arrived at a particular one. The moment I saw it, I knew that the search was over. It was strategically located between the I-95 interstate highway and the turnpike (toll highway). After taking a tour of the home, we were pleased with everything except the price, which was a bit on the high side. However, what made the decision to buy even more convincing was the drama that unfolded with Julianne, my daughter, who was less than two years old at the time. She was running throughout the house, having a wonderful time. However, after we were through with the tour, she started crying because she did not want to leave. Out of all the homes that we had seen that day, this was the only one that she was attached to. When I saw what had transpired, I knew right away that this was the assurance I needed to seal the deal. Once again, I was reminded of another biblical quote, "A little child shall lead them." Well, there could be other factors, but that's a good way to interpret it. With that said, I went ahead and made a down payment of five thousand dollars to start the process.

However, this transaction amplified my financial problems as they pertained to my outstanding credit card debts. In other words, this additional debt was financed by a credit card as well. In hindsight, this was surely not a sound financial decision, but sometimes "a man's gotta do

## Chapter 9

what a man's gotta do." In hindsight, this was surely not a sound financial decision, but sometimes "a man's gotta do what a man's gotta do." For me to be qualified for the mortgage, I needed to reduce my outstanding credit card debt by a substantial amount, but there was no way this would be possible with our current income. With that said, I quickly erased the thought of owning a home from my mind, at least for the moment. However, my optimism was rekindled when Ed, my Illinois friend, contacted me to see how life was going in the Sunshine State. One conversation led to the next, and I told him that I had seen a house in Port St. Lucie that was well suited for my family. I remember he said something to the effect of, "Have you closed on it yet?"

I responded casually, saying, "I have too much outstanding credit card debt." I did so in a casual manner because I was not asking Ed for any assistance. The last thing I wanted to do was to inflate my debt even further.

I was surprised when he said, "Desmond, if you really need this home and think that you can afford it, I will help you to pay down some of your outstanding debt, and you can pay me back later." I replied with a casual okay and continued with our general how-is-life-going conversation.

After we were through conversing, he said, "How much and to whom should I make out the check?" Immediately it dawned on me that Ed was not kidding. I hesitated for a moment because we had not yet figured out the exact amount or any repayment plan. Moreover, we needed some form of written agreement first. With that said, we discussed the terms and the other stipulations. After getting our signed agreement out of the way, Ed furnished me with a check, which I used to relinquish a portion of my outstanding credit card debt. This is why I would like to take this opportunity to say a special thank you to Ed for his thoughtfulness and extraordinary generosity in this regard.

Despite the overwhelming financial concerns, the real joy I felt when I used my own key to open the door to my own home was one of the happiest days of my life. To just stand there and reminisce on what I had been through, especially the many homeless days I spent while living with my mother, helped me to realize and to appreciate the wonderful blessings of God.

Okay, let me not get too carried away with becoming a homeowner because here comes the second unforeseen event that I warned you about earlier. My family's financial outlook was further complicated when I heard the unofficial, through-the-grapevine news that Adelphia would be taken over by Comcast, and the possibility of layoffs was imminent. In fact, it was a given that the division I worked for would be the first to suffer significant layoffs. It was only a matter of when we would receive the official confirmation.

One could only imagine how stressful the situation had become. I started thinking about the possibility of losing my first home to foreclosure. This was the first time in my life that I could associate my headaches and heartburn as being stress-related. The constant headaches and heartburn problems started to take a toll on my academic performance. I was unable to concentrate because my mind was always wandering off performing survival "what if" analysis. Besides, my academic time was now being consumed by other things, such as a job search and interviews. Searching for work had become more or less a full-time job!

Chapter 9

It appeared as though finding a job and winning the lottery had the same probability. At least from my perspective.

The third and final unforeseen event occurred when the painful heartburn that I had suffered while living with my former foster parents resurfaced. The pain and the side effects were too much to ignore, so I decided to consult a physician. After explaining my constant headaches and heartburn problems to Dr. R. D. Secontine, he looked at me and said, "You are a young man, what is going on in your life to be causing you so much stress?" I explained to him the things that were happening and the domino effect that could occur if I did not find a job very soon. He then suggested that I should think about postponing my studies because if I continued in this manner, my health could further deteriorate and the likelihood of my developing a stomach ulcer was highly probable.

During the evaluation process, Dr. Secontine made two statements that resonate in mind to this very day. First, he said, "According to the results of your blood test, it appeared as though at some point in your life, your body was constantly fighting off infections." He then followed up by asking, "Was there a point in your life that you can remember suffering from any infectious disease?" Although I surmised that this was a direct result of the environment my brother and I had been placed in while living with our former foster parents, for some unknown reason, I decided not to convey any of that to him. However, his inquiry helped me to understand the exact reason why my brother and I had suffered from all those painful lumps at our groins and under our armpits. Our bodies were continually fighting off infections that were attributable to working in maggot-infested chicken coops and pigpens barefoot and with many open wounds, especially those on our feet. I have outlined this condition in volume 2 of my autobiography.

The second statement that got my attention was when he acknowledged that the doctor-patient relationship is not what it used to be. He was referring to his earlier years. He continued by saying that, today, healthcare providers are treating the system like a cookie-cutter operation in which doctors are not being allowed enough consultation time with their patients. He concluded by saying that the entire healthcare process has been transformed into a money-making scheme. At the time, I did not understand much of what he was saying, however, the more I experienced the granular aspects of the healthcare system, the clearer Dr. Secontine's point became.

**The Bitter Pill**

At first, the thought of ignoring Dr. Secontine's advice concerning my academic goal was at the forefront of my mind; however, after being reminded that I was now a husband and a father, I decided to heed his advice. Besides, the severe headaches and constant heartburn were simply too much for me to ignore. Also, I was even more concerned that the severe heartburn I had suffered while living with my former foster parents would return. Today, I can assure you that I am very grateful for the time and effort that Dr. Secontine dedicated to my behalf. It allowed me to think about my priorities and act accordingly.

In addition to the doctor's advice, the results of that semester underscored the need for me to take immediate action as it pertained to my health. With that said, I reluctantly placed my academic career on hold indefinitely.

## Chapter 9

My illness had deprived me of the ability to put forth my best academic work, as indicated by my scorecard below. My poor academic performance was also highlighted in a concerted manner by my professor, which was quite the opposite of what I was accustomed to hearing. I can assure you that this was the most difficult decision I had to make concerning my academic career

As it relates to my academic setback, the dream is still within reach because I am a true believer in lifelong learning. Moreover, education and knowledge acquisition should never be treated as outdated or a thing of the past. This life experience helped me to understand and to sympathize with those who have suffered misfortunes or had to deal with unfortunate situations that hindered or, in some instances, caused them to terminate their academic careers or other important personal aspirations.

Let me say this, if it were not for that horrible heartburn I suffered throughout my childhood, there is a strong probability that I would have ignored the doctor's advice, and my dissertation topic would have been, "I gave it my all." In spite of the humor, I must also emphasize that my life's experiences concerning illness, layoffs, and financial turbulence are no different from that of the average

Term: Spring 2005
**Academic Standing:** Withdrawn

| Subject | Course | Level | Title | Grade | Credit Hours | Quality Points | R |
|---------|--------|-------|-------|-------|--------------|----------------|---|
| DISS | 0710 | C3 | Decision Support Systems | B- | 3.000 | 8.10 | |
| DISS | 0810 | C3 | Prj/Decision Support Sys | B- | 4.000 | 10.80 | |

**Term Totals (Doctorate - CCE)**

| | Attempt Hours | Passed Hours | Earned Hours | GPA Hours | Quality Points | GPA |
|---|---|---|---|---|---|---|
| **Current Term:** | 7.000 | 7.000 | 7.000 | 7.000 | 18.90 | 2.70 |
| **Cumulative:** | 21.000 | 21.000 | 21.000 | 21.000 | 72.80 | 3.46 |

## Unforeseen Events

American family. In fact, this is what a large number of people living in the United States are facing daily, which is a far cry from the perception I had before migrating to the United States.

Okay, back to my job prospects. Just as the layoffs were whispered through the grapevine, so were they manifested when we received the news that everyone (including me) who worked out of the West Palm Beach corporate office was being laid off by the company. This event placed enormous pressure on my family because we had school, daycare, mortgage, student loans, car loans, credit cards, and a lot more outstanding debt on hand. If you think my stress level was high when the news was trickling through the grapevine, then can you imagine what it was like when the news came through the official channel? I am here to confirm that my stress reading was at its max. Although Adelphia had promised to give us twenty days prior to the actual layoffs going into effect, it was still a gut-wrenching feeling to go to work on a given day and noticed that an entire division was missing. Day after day, I would show up to work with no sense of purpose, only to weather the uncertainty and watch as the layoffs devoured the workers, division by division. It was as though hundreds of people had found themselves stranded in the middle of the ocean only to watch helplessly as their comrades were being picked off by hungry sharks.

However, the entire burden was lifted off my shoulders when I was offered a job with the St. Lucie County. Although I was very happy to be moving on, I did miss working with the team and the wonderful business intelligence opportunity I had with Adelphia Communications. And how could I ever forget the wonderful sendoff my coworkers and managers gave me? My director and the rest of the team members invited not just me but also my wife and daughter to join a goodbye luncheon at the renowned Cracker Barrel restaurant.

Once again, I would like to emphasize that my illness, stress, layoffs, and job uncertainties are a reflection of what many American families are facing daily due to financial and other uncontrollable dynamics. However, not everyone is as fortunate as I was to have found a job and avert many of the unintended consequences that come with not being employed for a substantial period.

**Stability for the Family**

Before I proceed to my next job, I decided to heed Aunt Lucy's advice, in which she reminded me on many occasions to take the actions that are in the best interest of my family even if they take precedence over the plans and wishes I had regarding her. With that in mind, I commenced the process of becoming a naturalized US citizen. Up to this point, I had hoped to spend two "short" years in the United States and then return to Jamaica. So much for that hope because I was now entering my sixteenth year in the United States of America.

# CHAPTER 10

# A JOB IN TIME SAVES NINE

Although the compensation was rather small (relatively speaking), this was no time for me to be fastidious. Moreover, this job opportunity quelled the uncertainty that hung over my family. With that said, I joined St. Lucie County's information technology workforce with much enthusiasm.

I received my preliminary training and onboarding from Xavier, who was very knowledgeable, but at the same time, quite humble. He was never too busy to help me get over the learning curve. Therefore, I would like to take this moment to say a big thank you to Xavier for his patience, kindness, and, most of all, his friendship.

Throughout my time at St. Lucie County, I also supported the public defender's information technology needs. I had the opportunity to report to Susan, who was the information technology director. There were times when I would go by her office while she was busy on the computer or talking on the phone. However, instead of saying, "I am busy; go make an appointment," she would say to the person to whom she was speaking, "Please hold for a minute," and then she would say to me, "Des, I will

## Chapter 10

be right with you, honey." It was a pleasure working with the public defender's office because the staff members were very pleasant and welcoming. They even asked me to join in their birthday celebrations. I remember the ladies who worked on the first floor would come by my office and say, "Come on, Desmond! You are one of us. Let's go upstairs for cake." So it is in this manner that I would like to challenge anyone who dares to say that people "can't have their cake and eat it too." I must emphasize that these small tangible and intangible outreaches make me want to get up and go to work every day.

However, that year, 2007, I found myself contemplating the idea of restarting my doctoral academic journey. However, while I was contemplating this idea, I heard a clear and concise voice insisting that I should commence the writing of my autobiography. But for many reasons most notably psychological fear, I decided not to heed the calling. Nonetheless, the voice was persistent, and that was when I decided to heed the calling and commenced the writing of my autobiography.

CHAPTER 11

# HER FINAL DESTINY

Just as I settled into my new job, my entire life was thrown into turmoil once more when, on May 3, 2006, I received a very unfortunate and gut-wrenching message that Aunt Lucy had passed away. At that very defining moment, I felt as though my life no longer had any meaning and the very reason for my existence had been taken away from me. It felt as though I had no one left who could truly understand my joy and my desire for greater accomplishments. It felt as though my one and only motivational factor had been taken away. I was devastated! Although she was ninety-one years old at the time of her passing, I still was unable to come to terms with reality. I had been hoping that she would be around because I was planning on visiting her more often when things got better financially. I really wanted to spend more time with her. It was twenty-two years prior to the date of her passing when I had found myself without a home, not even a distant relative to turn to for support. However, my sorrow and my hopelessness had been replaced with joy and optimism when, out of the kindness of her heart, Aunt Lucy extended unto me a perpetual invitation into her home and into her life. Her decision to welcome me into her home was not based on any

## Chapter 11

financial feasibility or any other selfish motive. Instead, it was based on her love and never-ending compassion. Every day I have to remind myself that when I needed someone to love and care for me throughout my darkest hours, Aunt Lucy was there for me.

When I needed a home, Aunt Lucy swung her doors wide open and welcomed me into her home and into her life. When I needed food, she fed me. When I needed clothes, she clothed me. And, most importantly, it was through these acts of kindness that she taught me the true meaning of fostering. Although I was once a total stranger to her, that did not stop her from pouring out her heart and soul to provide for me in every way possible. She did everything possible so that I could be the person I am today.

At first, I did not understand the breadth and depth of Aunt Lucy's love and compassion. However, all that was manifested throughout the writing of my autobiography, especially when I had an opportunity to compare and contrast her actions with those of my former foster parents. My former foster parents instilled in me hard work, but it was Aunt Lucy who instilled in me the values that are associated with hard work. Today, I can truly acknowledge how fortunate I am to have had someone so special in my life. I could keep going on . . . and on, but I know you understand by now that Aunt Lucy was more than just another person whom I met as I traversed life's journey. I simply could not have asked anything more of her. Finally, I would like to quote a phrase from the United States Declaration of Independence by saying unequivocally that Aunt Lucy gave me a second chance to "life, liberty, and the pursuit of happiness."

My success can be attributed to the grace of God and the tangible and intangible means provided unto me by Aunt Lucy and the many other wonderful individuals and credible institutions of Jamaica and the United States of America. Looking back, I can genuinely say that the generous kindness of many has made my life whole. Therefore, I would like to use this opportunity to encourage everyone, more so those who are being or have been oppressed, please do not give up on your dreams because, with God, all things are possible. No matter where you find yourself in life, it is through hard work and perseverance that you can make it happen.

Before I bring this chapter to a close, I would like to express my sincere thanks and gratitude to Tracy Ann, my foster mother's great grandniece, for her thoughtfulness and the overwhelming compassion she bestowed unto Aunt Lucy. Her actions were even more apparent throughout the times I was away in the United States pursuing my academic studies. I did not have to worry because she would put forth the time and effort to make sure that Aunt Lucy's needs were met. I could always count on her to let me know how Aunt Lucy was doing. In fact, she contacted me two days before Aunt Lucy's passing and told me that I needed to come and visit Aunt Lucy because she did not think that Aunt Lucy could hold out any longer. Unfortunately, Aunt Lucy passed away before I had an opportunity to visit her and to bid her my final goodbye.

Now that my foster mother had passed, I needed to come to terms with not having her around anymore. I can assure you that this was very difficult for me to accept in the initial stage. However, seeing that my family is always my highest priority (which Aunt Lucy reminded me of on

## Chapter 11

several occasions), I decided to continue with the essential naturalization process. After filling out many INS forms and attending several in-person interviews, the process finally concluded on June 14, 2006, when I became a naturalized citizen of the United States of America.

# CHAPTER 12

# LIBERTY FOR ONE

After working for almost two years for St. Lucie County, I decided to accept a job with Liberty Medical Supply. Although I had been happy working for the county, Liberty made me an offer I simply could not refuse. This was the first time that I would be able to pay my bills without the need to subsidize my income with credit cards. So, from a financial perspective, I was sort of "liberated." With that said, I tendered my resignation to St. Lucie County. However, my managers and coworkers did not just say goodbye and good luck. No sir! Instead, they threw me a wonderful and memorable sendoff that involved a luncheon, cake, and ice cream too.

On September 4, 2007, I commenced working as a business systems analyst with Liberty. I enjoyed working with all my Liberty coworkers. However, I would like to say a special thank you to Jamie for being a kind and thoughtful coworker. She and I shared one office and worked together on several projects. Whenever I was experiencing a technology problem that was caused mostly by a simple oversight on my part (one of those self-inflicted wounds), she would come by and said, "Desmond, Desmond," then she would use the mouse and, with one or

## Chapter 12

two clicks followed by a couple of keystrokes, voilà! the problem would disappear. Whenever she was experiencing similar problems, I would do likewise. This is why having a coworker who cares makes a big difference, especially in the information technology field. But most importantly, I am very grateful for the uplifting quotes and Bible verses she shared with me.

Everything was going well at Liberty until another unforeseen event threw a couple of monkey wrenches into the works. Everything came to a halt when Medco took over Liberty and implemented several changes. Medco acquired Liberty Medical and was in the process of integrating both companies. Layoffs and consolidations were taking place, mostly at the top tier of the organization. However, those actions did send panic waves rippling down the lower tiers as well. After having learned my lesson at Adelphia Communications, I took the proactive approach and commenced the daunting task of job-hunting once more. After contacting many recruiters and attending several interviews, a breakthrough came when a recruiter contacted me via the phone. The recruiter forwarded me a copy of the job description and, after reviewing the requirements, I decided to move forward with an interview.

On August 21, 2008, I was contacted by a person who introduced himself as the director of business intelligence and e-business systems from *Company Zen*. *Company Zen* is an alias that I will use when referring to this company. After approximately thirty-five minutes of discussion, the person concluded the phone conversation and screening process. I was not too optimistic that I would receive a follow-up interview because of my lack of experience with respect to a specific software application.

However, to my surprise, I received an email from the recruiter in which she attached a copy of the director's response. The exact response was, "I like Desmond. He has a great 'can do' attitude." From my perspective, it was a joy and a privilege to be considered in such regard.

Approximately a week later, I was allowed to attend an in-person interview with *Company Zen*. This was the most comprehensive and time-consuming one-day interview I had ever attended.[6] After the interview, I felt very confident that I would receive positive feedback. However, this job was located some ninety-five miles away from home, which could turn out to be a five-hour daily commute (due to traffic). However, finding a place to live became paramount when on August 29, 2008, *Company Zen* made me an official offer, which I accepted. Not only was I being offered a much sought-after job, but I also received a significant salary increase and a sign-on bonus. Shortly after that, I received these kind words from the recruiter: "Thank you for being such a great candidate to work with. I am sure you will have a great career at [*Company Zen*]." Well, I thought so, too, but once again, if I could only see the future.

With no hesitation, I tendered my resignation from Liberty. Once again, my managers and coworkers organized

---

6 The Interview itinerary is as follows:
Date: Tuesday, August 26, 2008
01:00–1:45 p.m.   Person#1 Business Intelligence Analyst Sr.
01:45–2:30 p.m.   Person#2 Business Intelligence Analyst Sr.
02:30–03:00 p.m.  Person#3 Web Developer Sr.
03:00–03:45 p.m.  Person#4 Dir, BI&E Business Systems

## Chapter 12

for me a wonderful and memorable sendoff luncheon at one of the local restaurants.

But wait! I had not yet found a place to live in Ft. Lauderdale, so I needed to act quickly. However, I did not have to exert too much effort because I remember that Leighton, my foster mother's grandnephew, was currently living in Ft. Lauderdale. With that in mind, it was just a matter of giving him a call. As I outlined in volume 2, Leighton helped to reunite me with my biological family, including my mother and my sisters. With that said, I gave him a call and explained my need to him. With no hesitation, he said, "No problem man, you can come by anytime." So, after some seventeen years of leaving Jamaica, we finally met up once more. This arrangement was a blessing for me because it saved me the hassle of relocating my family to Ft. Lauderdale, especially not knowing how this job prospect would unfold.

# CHAPTER 13

# CONVERGENCE OF THE PAST AND THE PRESENT

**B**efore I get too excited and start chirping about this exciting business intelligence analyst career opportunity, I would like to share with you an important revelation that brought back vivid memories of my most emotional, fearful, and traumatic childhood experiences. At first, I was unable to appreciate the significance of this experience because I saw myself as a victim rather than understanding the message being conveyed. This traumatic experience was necessary because, without it, I would most likely have lived my entire life and not been able to identify with the psychological effects that are associated with a child, more so those concerning the children that were placed in my former foster parents' care. I was unaware that this experience was predestined and that it was meant to open my eyes to the root cause of my brother's lifelong psychological struggles, specifically those he incurred while living with our foster parents. This is just a preview of what is to come. I will provide the details shortly. To understand the full scope concerning my former foster parents, please refer to volume 2 of my autobiography.

## Chapter 13

Okay, back to the progress of my newly found job. On September 15, 2008, I set out for my new job with much enthusiasm and optimism. I was overwhelmed with joy, knowing that I finally had received a job in which I would be able to gain much information technology knowledge by assuming new and exciting roles. Besides, the compensation would allow me to start paying more than just the minimum on my outstanding debts. I was really looking forward to a long and prosperous career with this company. Who knows, I could end up retiring from this company. Well, that was what I thought. I even went as far as to put the writing of my autobiography on hold indefinitely so that I could divert all my attention to my new business intelligence analyst job. Okay, I do realize that I should have slowed down on my future plans because this excitement did not translate into the good fortune I had hoped for. Well, I should not have been imitating the man who was about to demolish his small barns and replace them with bigger ones not knowing what tomorrow will be (Bible reference). This experience reminded me exactly how I felt the day I was transferred from the orphanage into my first foster parents' care. This analogy will become apparent shortly.

Before I continue with this job progress, I would like to tell you a little story about my appendix. The wonderful joy and happiness I had concerning my newly found career were disrupted when, out of nowhere, I became severely ill. It started out with a slight abdominal pain, which I ignored completely. My concern was never to let anything get in the way of or derail this exciting opportunity. Not even illness. However, on October 30, 2008, I started experiencing severe abdominal pain, which I chose to ignore. Even the coworkers I ate lunch with were not aware of the severity of my illness and started poking fun at me. They were implying in a jovial manner that it was the goat (curried goat meat) I ate for lunch that was gouging me in my stomach with its horns. Not knowing the severity of my illness either, I started drinking quite a bit of hot ginger beverage, which at first appeared to be working. The pain subsided to the point that I thought all was well. However, on November 4, 2008, I was feeling sick, with severe pain radiating throughout my abdomen. Associating this pain with my appendix was the last thing on my mind. Right away, I started taking all sorts of medication for gas and indigestion discomfort. Most Jamaicans, especially in the rural areas, attribute any and every pain to excessive gas discomfort. It does not matter if you are feeling the pain in your head, stomach, yes, or even in your ankles! The first remedy that is applied is some form of gas-relief medication or therapy. This philosophy remains true in all circumstances unless it is aggressively disproved by a medical expert. Anyway, I left work at approximately 7:45 p.m., and with the guiding hands of the Lord, I made it home safely.

That night was a defining moment for the nation. It was democracy at its finest. The election process for a new president was underway. Therefore, the very thought of being admitted to the hospital was the last thing on my mind. I was hoping and praying that would not be the case because I did not want to miss out on this historic moment. I had come home hoping to be glued to the television but, instead, I found myself hunched over on the floor due to excruciating pain. I can say with all surety that I felt as though I were breathing my last breath. That was when it

# Chapter 13

dawned on me that my illness seemed to be more than just gas pain.

**I Think It's Time to Go to the Emergency Room**

At approximately 11:00 p.m., the pain became unbearable. Unable to stand upright, I crawled on my hands and knees to Leighton's room. I knocked on the door, and he came out and saw me on the floor. He picked me up off the floor but discovered that I was unable to stand upright. With no further hesitation, he said, "Come, man! You need fi go to di hospital." He placed me in his car, but I was unable to sit upright, so I just hunched over on the floor. Let's forget about the Florida "click it or ticket" law because I was much safer on the floor of the car than I would have been sitting upright and being secured with a seatbelt.

The minute we arrived at the Florida Medical Center emergency room, the attendant, a young woman, commenced the check-in process by asking me several questions. Leighton became my spokesperson and facilitator because I was in too much pain to go through a rigorous Q&A session. I am quite sure that she was working as fast as she could, but from my perspective, she was treating the situation as if I were there for a general checkup that did not require any sense of urgency. Wouldn't it be a smoother process if everyone had a biometric chip that could be read electronically? This would negate the possibility of a dying person (like me) being subjected to so many darn questions! Especially a simple question that had to do with having or not having insurance! Thank God, my wife had added me to her insurance because if that were not the case, then the outcome would have been much different.

That is, instead of lying in a hospital bed recouping, my friends and loved ones would have gathered at my graveside singing the chorus from the most notable funeral song, "Yes, we'll gather at the river, the beautiful, the beautiful river." Okay, a little too much speculation, but I believe you get the point. After the check-in process was completed, I was told to have a seat in the waiting area.

Finally! At the end of eternity, I saw a woman coming toward me with a wheelchair. I wanted to pick myself up off the floor and jump into the wheelchair, but I realized that it was just a figment of my imagination. In fact, Leighton had to pick me up off the floor and place me in the chair. I was then wheeled inside and placed in a room.

**Could It Be My Appendix and Not Gas Pain?**

After the nurse was through with the preliminaries, the doctor came into the room and commenced the examination by asking me a few questions. I am not sure what my responses were because I was in too much pain to talk. However, I was quickly brought back to consciousness when he pressed down on my lower abdomen. This action triggered a pain that radiated throughout my entire nervous system. All I could do was scream. And that was when I heard him said, "Yep, it is your appendix. You will have to undergo surgery."

After a series of diagnoses, the surgeon told me that my surgery would have to be treated differently from the normal appendicitis operation because my appendix was inflamed and could rupture any moment. I can assure you that those weren't comforting words at all. Nonetheless, I tried to stay calm throughout the process. When all the

## Chapter 13

tests and retests were completed, on Thursday, November 6, 2008, I was wheeled into surgery. Oops, not so fast! Just as I was about to be taken into surgery, a woman came into the room and started harassing me for money. She demanded a whopping six-hundred-dollar upfront payment. She told me that this amount must be paid in full before the surgery. I guess she did not want to take any chances and needed her money just in case the surgeon experienced one of those "oops" moments. Once again, even while I was lying on my sickbed, I had no other choice but to resort to my trusted Chase Mastercard. I was in so much pain that I did not even question the reason why they were charging six hundred dollars upfront. Hello! Who dares to say, "Money can't buy you life?" Just kidding, I know it can't, but it sure felt that way at the time.

When it was all over, on Saturday, November 8, 2008, my wife, my daughter, and my mother-in-law came by and took me home. Not realizing the side effects of surgery, I tried to convince my wife that I was well enough to go back to work in a couple days. She reminded me that I would need at least two weeks of recovery time before I could go back to work. My wife is quite familiar with the recovery process based on her experience working with patients who have undergone surgery. Moreover, her advice was most apparent when I got up the following morning and found that I was unable to step down off the bed due to excruciating pain. I had no idea that the very basic things, such as a sneeze, cough, or laughter, that are part of everyday life, could have caused me so much pain. I was afraid that if I sneezed or coughed, the staples that the doctor used to stitch my wound would go flying from my stomach. However, I must admit that the reason why I was quite eager to

## Convergence of the Past and the Present

go back to work was the fact that I was overly concerned about my lucrative business intelligence career. Instead of taking the time to celebrate life and to appreciate what the Lord had done for me, there I was worried about a job! This is proof that my priorities were certainly not in the correct order!

**Okay, Let's Get Back to Work**

After approximately twelve days of recovery, the doctor removed the staples and provided me with a return-to-work permission slip. Although I was experiencing mild pain, from a mental point of view I was more than ready to go back to work. On November 18, 2008, I returned to work with much enthusiasm, knowing that the appendix drama was finally over. However, after the first few hours of sitting upright, I realized that I was not quite ready for an eight-hour shift. Once again, I was reminded that pain and gain are very much interrelated.

**It's the Phone; Who Could It Be?**

Well, forget about the "pain and gain" philosophy I just mentioned, because there was much psychological pain coming my way. After receiving a phone call from my director, he summoned me into his office. The minute I stepped into his office, I was greeted with a barrage of verbal insults followed by the worst performance evaluation of my life. I can assure you that the psychological pain I felt that day was much worse than the appendicitis ordeal I had just experienced. At that very moment, I experienced vivid flashbacks of my traumatic childhood years.

This experience brought back many years of psychological pain that I had tried to erase from my memory!

I have included a copy of the performance review (Appendix A), but I have redacted the company and the director's name because it is not about the subjects but, instead, it is about the experience that opened my eyes to the psychological struggles that my brother had endured his entire life. Therefore, this experience was worth the minor inconvenience I had to tolerate. This incident opened my eyes to the fact that my past experiences were not coincidental or a result of misfortune. However, through them, the Lord has allowed me to address the injustice that is associated with the broader context of this world.

**Psychological Resurgence**

I hope that you had a chance to review my interesting performance evaluation because I will now provide you with the details of the unexpected revelation that made me realize that I was once again reliving my most fearful and traumatic childhood experience.

For reasons unknown to me, my coworker, who had been assigned to mentor me throughout the onboarding period, would, on several occasions, insult and humiliate me. Shortly after that, my manager started directing similar behavior at me as well. Nonetheless, I thought that if given more time to prove myself, this situation would eventually work itself out. However, over time, the constant insults and humiliations brought back those painful and frightening childhood memories my brother and I had endured while living with our former foster parents. As for me, the real question was this: How could it be that after

## Convergence of the Past and the Present

twenty-seven years of not being subjected to such an environment, I was once again reliving those painful and fearful memories of my childhood?

Although I am unable to provide a conclusive answer to this question, I do believe that after experiencing many of the fearful "shock and awe" psychological flashbacks, I started exhibiting the very same withdrawn syndromes I had while living with my former foster parents. The two most obvious were not being able to communicate and not being able to make eye contact with the person to whom I was speaking. Besides, I found myself unable to process basic instructions due to extreme fear. Throughout my childhood years, my brother and I were forbidden from indulging in any form of communication with our foster parents, more so our foster mother. We were also forbidden from making eye contact with our foster mother. We had to look off to the side or to the ground while she was speaking or reprimanding us. Even though we did all the things deemed acceptable, none of that mattered because we were shunned and addressed as dogs and scavengers for no apparent reason other than we were considered orphans. Therefore, these flashback experiences made it quite difficult for me to indulge in what should have been normal communication with my coworker and manager. This explains the reason why my coworker would remind me on several occasions that I needed to look directly at her throughout our conversation. She would say, "I am over here, not over there!" Sometimes she would say, "I cannot understand what you are saying if you do not look directly at me while you are speaking."

The most obvious incident happened one day when my coworker snatched a computer keyboard from my hands

## Chapter 13

and, in a frustrated manner, shouted, "You are unable to use a basic keyboard!" She resorted to such a measure because she was providing me with the access code to a computer, and all I needed to do was to type each character while she repeated them to me verbally. She had repeated herself several times, but I was unable to process her instructions due to the extreme psychological fear that had consumed me. After several attempts, the computer employed the lockout security measure, thus causing her to snatch the computer keyboard from my hands. Immediately after that, I found myself bracing for a head bashing, but that did not happen because it was all in my mind.

After examining this incident thoroughly, I realized that my behavior was indeed a reflection of the psychological fear that I had developed while living with my former foster parents. This experience was identical to what took place when my foster mother summoned me to one of her regimental study sessions. The minute I stood before her, extreme fear would cause me to panic and, eventually, my brain would shut down. Not only that, but my slow-paced learning had become an irritant to her, thus causing her to lose her patience. And from that point forward, she would resort to inflicting the most painful and humiliating forms of physical (including being hit on the head repeatedly) and psychological punishment on me because I was unable to read, write, or comprehend her instructions. I have covered this extensively in volume 2.

Before this manifestation, I was unaware that the traumatic experiences of my childhood could have had such a profound effect on my behavior as an adult. I thought that those experiences would have faded away over time. However, today, I am convinced that the traumatic experiences of a person's childhood do contribute directly and indirectly to his or her behavior when confronted with the same or a similar experience thereafter. This experience has helped me to understand that even as an adult, my brother's psychological pain was most certainly a reflection of the traumatic experiences he had endured while living with our former foster parents.

Irrespective of my childhood recurrence, I would like to use this experience as a source of strength. Also, I would like to encourage those of us who have gone through or find ourselves going through similar situations to please foster those thoughts that lift you up, comfort you, and seek forgiveness, not those that seek revenge through anger or hate. This philosophy is what has helped me to forgive my former foster parents, especially my former foster mother. Although at times it may seem justifiable not to forgive, I would like to encourage you (and myself alike) to think and act otherwise.

As a child, I had no other choice but to endure the constant physical and psychological abuse directed at me by my former foster parents. However, in this instance, I realized that I did not have to subject myself to such an environment, especially one in which I found myself reliving the most painful memories of my childhood. With that said, I went ahead and tendered my resignation from Company Zen.

Before I continue, I would like to point out that this situation was most likely triggered due to my inability to comprehend at the desired pace, thus causing my coworker and manager to display such behavior toward me. This assertion is based on my performance review, as outlined in Appendix A. Although this was a very painful experience, I came to

## Chapter 13

realize that my inability to learn at the average pace has become one of my most painful lifelong limitations. Today I realize that with a family and age catching up with me, I am no longer able to engage in my usual all-night study ritual. This limitation has undoubtedly become my "thorn in the flesh" (biblical reference) weakness. Well, I am not sure if my experience measures up to this biblical phrase, but at the time, it felt like a painful thorn in my flesh. By the way, I believe that every one of us has a thorn that we have to live with. Okay, I believe I have said enough about thorns, so let us smile and move on.

Before I bring this chapter to a close, I would like to fast-forward and explain how I unintentionally carried over this traumatic experience to my next job. Throughout the early stage of my second employment with Bank of America, my natural reaction was to avoid any and all direct conversation with my manager, John Barger, as a way of negating any possibility of reliving the traumatic experiences I had been through while working at Company Zen. Even when I was forced to communicate with my manager via the phone, I would do everything possible not to let him speak or try to end the conversation, hoping that I would negate any possibility of him ridiculing or humiliating me. However, instead of treating the situation as a deficiency in my ability to communicate or merely reprimanding me because he has the authority to do so, in a concerned and thoughtful manner, John brought it to my attention throughout a one-on-one discussion. Although at the time I did not understand the reason for such behavior, I did shortly after that. I also realized that I need to be aware of my actions and to ensure that they were not a reflection of my past traumatic

*Convergence of the Past and the Present*

experiences, especially those of my childhood. Although I am speaking from years of personal experience, I also understand that my advice in this regard is much easier said than done.

Moreover, I have witnessed firsthand the emotional toll this childhood experience had on my only brother; a toll that contributed to his untimely passing. In the end, there was no one there to save him because his unyielding cry for justice had become an echo that only he alone could hear. This is one more reason why I would like to take this opportunity to say a special thank you to John Barger for his overwhelming thoughts and consideration, especially throughout such a crucial period in my life. I would only hope and pray that we have more people-person managers in the world who are like John.

## CHAPTER 14

# THE MEMORABLE 360-JOURNEY OF MY CHILDHOOD

After having gone through the most recent traumatic experience outlined in the previous chapter, I found myself unable to sleep. In addition to my insomnia problem, I started to experience heartburn and constant headaches. I was quite fearful that the excruciating heartburn that had plagued me for several years while living with my former foster parents would resurface. After reminding myself that I had little or no control over my psychological encounters, I decided to embrace my fears by taking a trip down memory lane. After discussing my therapeutic adventure with my family, in February 2009, I packed a small carry-on suitcase with a couple of pieces of clothes and a couple dozen Zantac, Prilosec, and Advil capsules, and I boarded a flight destined for Montego Bay, Jamaica.

For you to put this chapter into perspective, I would recommend that you read the first two volumes of my autobiography. Otherwise, you can proceed. However, a few references might be a bit difficult for you to contextualize.

## Chapter 14

The minute I landed in Jamaica, I felt as though a great load had been lifted off my shoulders. Immediately, I commenced what I would describe as the 360-journey of my Jamaican life. I intended to visit family, friends, and institutions that had played vital roles in my life, especially throughout my childhood and adolescent years. Usually, one of my first stops would be to visit my Aunt Lucy. However, seeing that she was no longer with me in this life, my first visit was with my eldest sister, Inez. It was throughout times such as these that I really missed my foster mother, and found myself yearning for her most comforting and uplifting words. After spending the first night with my sister, the following day, I continued my historical 360-journey and made my second stop at the Garland Hall Children's Home, the orphanage in Anchovy, St. James. Just a reminder, this orphanage acted as a revolving door for my brother and me over a three-year period, which I have documented in volume 1 of my autobiography.

I took my niece Donnett with me so that she could have a firsthand view of my childhood home. After some thirty-plus years, I had the opportunity of taking a grand tour of the facility that had once been my home. I even

Front view of the Garland Hall Children's Home.

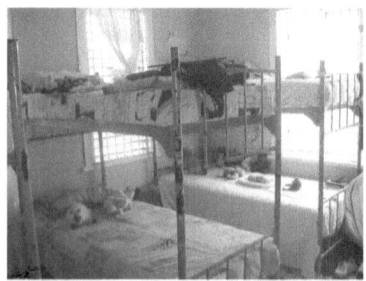

The top left and the bottom right bunk beds provided me with many warm and cozy nights' sleep

found myself sitting in the very spot where I used to spend many days looking out for my mother. I remember missing out on several meals because I thought that my mother would pass by, and I would never get a chance to see her again. However, if you recall (as outlined in volume 1), it was just a prank that had been orchestrated by the older boys. Moreover, at the time, I had no recollection of my mother. Therefore, my mother could have passed by the orphanage one thousand times, and I would not have recognized her.

Here I am, sitting in the very spot overlooking the roadway, trying to recreate my memorable "Looking out for my mother" episode.

## Chapter 14

I had the privilege of talking with Ms. Woodit, the director of the orphanage, and a number of the staff members. Throughout our conversation, I asked her if she knew Auntie (the former director), and she replied, "You mean Ms. Edna Harty?" It was enlightening for me to finally know her name because all this time, I was accustomed to addressing her as Auntie. In fact, all of the children who were residing at the orphanage addressed her as Auntie. Ms. Woodit also told me that Ms. Harty was retired and living at Mount Carey. I am very familiar with the Mount Carey district because I used to attend the Mount Carey Baptist Church while I was residing at the orphanage. After my lengthy discussion with Ms. Woodit, I went to Mount Carey to look for Auntie. On my way, I stopped by the kindergarten and Anchovy Primary School, where I had attended classes briefly while residing at the orphanage.

My next stop was at the Mount Carey Baptist Church. The image below is a partial view of the megachurch I alluded to earlier (volume 1) while discussing the memorable days I spent at the orphanage. I can still hear the

Anchovy kindergarten. This is where I attended school briefly while living at the Garland Hall Children's Home.

My first-grade classroom at Anchovy Primary. This is where I spent a couple of months before being transferred from the orphanage to my first foster parents.

harmonic voices and the melodious tunes echoing from the choir and the magnificent pipe organ.

My next task was to locate Ms. Edna Harty (Auntie). After asking several of the Mount Carey residents for her whereabouts, I finally found her relaxing at home in the cool hills of Mount Carey. She had been the director of the Garland Hall Children's Home for over forty years. Throughout such time, she had overseen the transition of many, many children, including my brother and me. I could not resist the temptation, so I am going to let you have a sneak peek.

Mount Carey Baptist Church.

After saying goodbye to Auntie, I was a bit tired, so I went back to Inez's home and called it a day. However, before you and I proceed to the next phase of my 360-journey, I would like to update you on the most recent news I received concerning Ms. Edna Harty. She passed away four years later, in 2013. I had hoped to visit her a second time so that we could spend more time catching up on past memories. Nonetheless, may her soul be comforted as she bid her final farewell to her exhaustive but impactful labor of this life.

After some forty-plus years of directorship, Ms. Edna Harty (Auntie) retired and enjoyed her youthful years in the cool hills of the Mount Carey district.

## Chapter 14

The following day Paulette (my sister) and Donnett (my niece) accompanied me as I journeyed to Westmoreland in search of Aunt Nell. I had no idea if I would recognize her because I had not seen her in approximately thirty-two years. In fact, the last time I had seen her was when we became homeless and were living on the mountain. And if you recall, we had our cover blown and had to cease living on the mountain. Also, shortly after leaving the mountain, the authorities removed my brother and me from our mother's care and transferred us back to the orphanage. The details of this episode are documented in volume 1 of my autobiography. Once again, after driving all over and making many inquiries, we finally found Aunt Nell and one of my cousins, Byron.

Aunt Nell (my mother's sister)

My sister, Paulette and our cousin, Byron (Aunt Nell's son)

My niece Donnette (Inez daughter)

After a short meet and greet, my aunt and cousin accompanied me to Darliston, where I used to live with my father. On the way, I made a stop at my mother's home. However, I found out that it was burnt down a couple

This is all that is left of my mother's home

of days prior. As you can see, only the foundation is left standing.

The infant school I attended briefly (more like four to six weeks) in 1976.

From there, we went to Darliston, where I located several people who were able to fill me in on my early childhood years and the time I spent with my father. I also visited the St. John's Infant school, where I had attended classes for a couple of weeks before I was removed by my father because attending school was in stark contrast to his Rastafarian doctrine. In fact, none of us (my brother or my twin sisters) were allowed to attend school because our father considered school to be an instrument of the Babylonian system (volume 1).

## Chapter 14

The little doggie was home alone. Notice how the little doggie bowl has taken a beating. It has more craters than planet Mercury.

Joy and two of her children, Monique, and Nathaneal.

On the next leg of my 360-journey, I visited my former foster parents' home. Although they had died, I was hoping to see their adopted son, Michael or their adopted daughter, Joy, and her husband and two children. However, no one was at home except for the little doggie.

Since their passing, I have kept in frequent contact with their adopted daughter, Joy and grandson, Christopher. Although Joy was not at home, later that day, I happened to meet up with her and her two wonderful children Monique, and Nathaniel, in Brown's Town, St Ann.

Her elder son Christopher was working in Kingston, Jamaica, so I did not get a chance to see him. As of our most recent conversation, he is now in Canada, pursuing another phase of his academic journey. It was always a joy to hear from him, especially when he updated me on his academic and career accomplishments. I am extremely proud of him!

Next, I visited one of the neighbors' homes to say hi to the children I had known throughout the time I was living with my former foster parents. The minute I arrived, I met a lady whom I remembered quite well because her parents and my former foster parents had been neighbors. Not only

## The Memorable 360-Journey of My Childhood

was she surprised to see me, but she said, "The only thing that is stuck in my head to this day is the crying I used to hear coming from you guys' being beaten every day." She was referring to the children, including me, who were being abused by my former foster parents. I was hoping that we could reminisce about other things and share a few laughs, but unfortunately that was not the case. Although she had been only a child at the time, it is quite telling that she was disturbed by the constant abuse that we (more so the foster children) had been subjected to at the hands of my foster parents. Even as an adult, she seemed to be emotionally distraught by what she had witnessed. I do understand her concern because, even to this very day, I am emotionally distraught as well.

The following day I visited the Stewart Town Primary School, formerly known as the Stewart Town All-Age School. This school is located in the parish of Trelawny. I attended this school for approximately five years and four months. My former foster mother was also a teacher and the acting vice-principal at this school. If you have already read volume 2 of my autobiography, then this reference should bring back many memories, including the unforgettable female shoe drama. Anyway, throughout my visit, I met two of the teachers, Ms. Bailey and Joseph. Ms. Bailey was my fourth-grade teacher and Joseph was my former classmate. They both are contributing to the community in a meaningful way through teaching.

The following day I went to Sawyers, where I spent my adolescent years with my wonderful, caring, and loving foster mother, Aunt Lucy. Just a quick reminder, Sawyers is a little farming district that is located in the parish of Trelawny. Usain Bolt, the world's fastest man, as per world

## Chapter 14

Stewart Town All Age School. This is where I completed my second through eighth grade school years.

My second-grade classroom. This is where my real academic life began. And yes! It is also where some interesting school drama unfolded most notable, the pair of female shoes I wore to school.

Sawyers All-Age School, where I completed the final six months of my ninth-grade academic year (1984).

records, is also a native of this parish. My first stop was at the Sawyers All-Age School. I had the opportunity to meet with the principal, Mrs. Golding, and several teachers. Mrs. Golding is the wife of Mr. Talbert Golding, who was the principal and also my ninth-grade teacher throughout the six months I attended this school.[7]

Next, I visited my once-upon-a-time "home sweet home," which is located in the little farming community of

---

[7] Here is a link to an article that best describes my former principal and ninth-grade teacher: (*http://old.jamaica-star.com/thestar/20090414/features/features2.html*). If this link does not work, please refer to The Memorable 360-Journey of My Childhood section located at the *www.fosteringthroughtheeyesofachild.net* website.

## Chapter 14

Here is a partial view of the land that I once used for farming vegetables. The Lord blessed it, and it yielded an abundance of vegetables, which I sold to the locals and used the proceeds to finance my academic expenses and other financial obligations.

This is Aunt Lucy's home, where I used to live.

Hope Gospel Hall is where I attended church of approximately eight years.

Burke, in Sawyers, Trelawny. Here is a glimpse of the land I used for growing vegetables. I hope you have not forgotten the vegetable business venture that I used to finance my academic career, as I outlined in detail in volume 2 of my autobiography.

The Hope Gospel Hall is where I used to attend Sunday school and other weekday services. I have especially vibrant memories of attending the young people's meetings.

My next stop was at the Albert Town Secondary School (now Albert Town High). This school is where Aunt Lucy pleaded on my behalf when she was told that there was no available space at the school for me. Her

## Chapter 14

Albert Town High school (formerly Albert Town Secondary) is still serving as a vital knowledge infusion to the community. As you can see, the motto speaks for itself.

relentless perseverance paid off when the school administrator finally heeded her plea and admitted me to the school. This academic and vocational institution is where I commenced my electrical installation career as well.

The next phase of my 360-journey took me to the Runaway Bay HEART Academy. To date, after thirty-two plus years, there have been significant improvements and staff changes. The training institution is still in full operation, providing hotel management training to residential and nonresidential trainees. The Runaway Bay HEART Academy added twenty-four more rooms to the hotel

Here is a snapshot (front view) of the Cardiff Hotel & Spa, once known as the Runaway Heart Hotel. This academic institution is where I completed my hotel management training program.

Side view of the Cardiff Hotel & Spa.

The newly added guest rooms at the Cardiff Hotel & Spa.

sector of the academy. After the expansion, the hotel now has a combined forty-four guest rooms.[8]

---

8 Looking for a vacation? Just wave the Google magic wand using the hotel name or go directly to the hotel website at *https://www.thecardiffhotel.com*. Additional information related to the HEART Trust NTA program can be found at *http://www.heart-nta.org/*.

## Chapter 14

The academic side of the Runaway Bay HEART Academy.

Here is a peek at the dormitory (dorm #6). I once occupied the left bottom bunk and Harry the left top bunk. I hope you have not forgotten the history of the bottom bunk and how I was being tagged with the "Small Boy" pet name. The details are covered in volume 2

After taking a tour of the Runaway Bay HEART Academy and the Cardiff Hotel & Spa, I visited Mrs. HoSang, who I would like to refer to as my "HEART mom." Her children are all grown up and on their own. Yolanda has completed her MD training and is now serving the parish of St. Ann. Today, the house is a lot quieter than when all of us were at home.

Mrs. HoSang (my HEART Mom) relaxing on her verandah enjoying the cool Cardiff Hall breeze.

Finally, or should I say last but certainly not least, I completed my 360-journey by stopping at the Donald Sangster International Airport in Montego Bay. I had the opportunity of

As you can see, Trevor and I were doing our best to recreate our airport cooking experience.

## Chapter 14

visiting with a number of my former coworkers. Most of them were no longer working directly with the Airports Authority of Jamaica due to the privatization venture. However, Trevor, one of my former coworkers and "executive chef," was still working for the airport. As I outlined in volume 2, Trevor and I had been employed by the Airports Authority of Jamaica in 1988. If you recall, it was during the 3:00 to 11:00 p.m. shift that Trevor would cook some of the most delicious meals. Yummy! He also gave me a jump start on the art of Jamaican cooking, for which I am really grateful. As you can see, Trevor and I were trying our best to recreate our airport cooking experience. However, the seasoning, oil, chicken, rice, and flour were all missing.

The airport was the last job I had before migrating to the United States of America. Before I bring this section to a close, I would also like to use this opportunity

Here is a partial view of the newly renovated Donald Sangster International Airport. It is undoubtedly like night and day when compared to the airport at which I once worked. I wish I had a before photo to show you.

to appreciate my fellow coworkers (as outlined in volume 2) for their guidance, generosity, and, most of all, their patience as they guided me throughout the learning process. Although I was the youngest and most likely the least experienced member of the team, that was not seen or used as a weakness against me. Instead, I was given the opportunity to develop my skills and to progress.

**The Sudden Loss of Loved Ones**

Before I proceed to the next phase of my life's journey, I would like to share with you the final chapter of Mr. and Mrs. HoSang's lives. Mr. HoSang's life was cut short when he was gunned down and passed away on March 24, 2012. I was deeply saddened by the sudden loss of someone who had been like a father to me over many years. It was and still is very difficult for me to understand. This incident is a manifestation of our unforgiving nature and the total disregard we have for human lives.

Two years later, Mrs. HoSang passed away on December 25, 2014. It was quite difficult to grasp because I had the opportunity to speak with her approximately two weeks before her passing. Throughout our conversation, we exchanged laughter as we caught up on old times. We also discussed plans for a family reunion the following year. Over the years I came to know Mrs. HoSang, I can truly say that people like her were placed on this earth for a special reason. Mr. and Mrs. HoSang welcomed me into their home and, above all, treated me like a son. Although they are no longer with me in this life, I can assure you that their heartfelt love and overwhelming compassion will never be forgotten.

*Chapter 14*

**Time to Turn the Page**

After a week of visiting with families, friends, and a number of prominent institutions that had fostered me throughout my childhood and adolescent years, I realized that it was time for me to take my life out of the "cool runnings, no problem man" island mode and return to the United States of America to be with my family. Although I missed my family very much, I was certainly not looking forward to resuming the stressful job search and the other ordeals that are associated with not having a full-time job. Just to be clear, I would like to point out that this ordeal was not exclusive to just me. In fact, millions of Americans were in the same, or worse, predicament. However, before I close this chapter, I would like to share with you a little phenomenon that I classify as the "mind over matter debacle." Do you realize that for the entire time that I was in Jamaica, I had not needed to take any of my stomach or headache medication (Zantac, Prilosec, or Advil)? Not only had I not needed to take any medication, but I also slept through the nights with no problem. Moreover, the thought of not having a job had long been dissipated from my mind, which is why I classified this phenomenon as the "mind over matter debacle."

This emotional life's journey had reminded me of how fortunate I was and how I should be more appreciative of my undeserved blessings. It made me realize that I should never again bind my heart to a job or any other material possession to the point that my life and the things I adored dearly became inseparable. Having the opportunity to visit the orphanage, which I once called home, made me realize how ungrateful I had become. I was reminded that I should be a lot more appreciative of my accomplishments because they had exceeded my wildest imagination. Moreover, I realized that losing a job or any other material possession should not take away or diminish my joy and optimism.

Today, I am very grateful for the overwhelming compassion that has been bestowed unto me by the outstretched arms of many strangers, including Aunt Lucy. I am also grateful for institutions such as the Garland Hall Children's Home, the Child Development Agency of Jamaica, and the many others that were there to facilitate my development needs. These individuals and institutions instilled in me the yearning desire to contribute time and resources to prevent less fortunate children from becoming unknown shadows of society. Unfortunately, my brother was one of the less fortunate children who fell victim to the unknown. The one regret I had regarding this trip was the fact that my brother's mental condition did not allow him to accompany me on this historic 360-journey. If this had not been the case, then we certainly would have had a lot to talk about as we reminisced about our childhood years.

# CHAPTER 15

# THE JOURNEY

After returning to the United States, I decided to go in search of aunt Nells daughter, Vyroline (Diana). After a phone call, we finally linked up, and she provided me with the address to her home. I was very excited to meet up with my cousin. As I outlined in volume 1, Diana and her siblings were with us throughout the challenging times we spent with our parents. She was

My cousin, Vyroline

also removed from her mother's care and transferred to the Garland Hall Memorial Children's Home. After our meet and greet, we bid each other goodbye, and I went home. This concluded my family search in the year 2009.

The following day I picked up where I had left off with my technology training and the tedious job search. However, after searching for a while with no success, I became a bit frustrated to the point that I found myself asking the Lord why I was unable to find a job. Why was it that even after acquiring all these academic credentials, I kept getting one rejection after another? Every time that I would

## Chapter 15

ask myself this very question, I always heard the same whispering voice saying to me, "You must resume the writing of your autobiography." Every time that I would put the writing of my autobiography aside, there was always a convincing voice that kept reminding me that I should not neglect this important calling. I had been ignoring this calling because of the psychological pain, especially when I reflected on the abuse my brother suffered at the hands of our former foster parents. However, I realized that if writing my autobiography could prevent one child from falling into the unknown shadows of society, then it would most certainly be worth the psychological pain I had to endure. If writing my autobiography helped to prevent one person, system, or nation from indulging in the deceptive behaviors that my former foster parents were guilty of, then it would most certainly be worth the time I had invested and the psychological pain I had endured. Finally, if writing my autobiography caused one person, system, or nation to turn to God and to cease actions that were harmful to humanity, then it would most certainly have achieved the broader objective. With that in mind, I decided to resume the writing of my autobiography.

**Let's Put the Future on Hold While I Revisit the Past**

Just when I thought that my childhood records were nowhere to be found, after some eight months of intense searching, Mrs. Riley, a representative of the Falmouth Child Development Agency division, contacted me with the much-anticipated news. She told me that she had located not just my file, but my brother's file as well. This was exciting news because I finally had the opportunity to

## The Journey

read what had been written concerning me for many years! I knew that it was not an easy task for Mrs. Riley because she had to have spent many long and tedious hours searching for our files. Before I proceed, I would like to take this opportunity to express my sincere gratitude to the CDA staff members at the Montego Bay division for allowing my sister, Inez, and my grandnephew, Omar, to assist with the tedious search of locating my file. However, after the Montego Bay division did not yield any result, the search was extended to the CDA office located in Falmouth, Trelawny, where Mrs. Riley and Ms. Minto went the extra mile to tolerate the dust and the humidity and located the needles in the haystack. Wouldn't this search have been a piece of cake if our files had been electronically stored and were retrievable with just a few keystrokes?

On December 8, 2009, I booked a round-trip ticket destined for Montego Bay, Jamaica. Finally, I had an opportunity to read for the very first time what had been written concerning my brother and me while we were in the care of the CDA. I was intrigued by the level of effort that the agency had put forth to document our lives from 1975 through to 1985 and 1987, respectively. This opportunity provided closure to many of my unanswered questions.

One of my most memorable experiences of this trip came on the very first day, while I was at the CDA office reading through my file. Just around noon, it started raining cats and dogs. We had to close the windows and doors because the rain started pouring into the office. If the office was equipped with an air conditioning system, it had to be broken because it was hot and humid inside the office. There was no escaping the humidity because even my file started to crumble. That was when I turned to Mrs. Riley

## Chapter 15

and asked her what had motivated her to choose this not-so-glamorous career and to tolerate such an unpleasant working environment. Without any hesitation, she said, "I chose this career because I have a passion for caring for children." I know that there had to be other intangible motivational factors than just money. This example is yet another reminder that Mrs. Riley is one of the few people willing to forgo financial gain and, yes, even a comfortable working environment because they cared deeply about the well-being of others, more so, the unfortunate children. I can relate to her in this regard because it was just like yesterday that I had found myself at the mercy of Aunt Lucy for my everyday survival needs and she had welcomed me with open arms and done everything possible to provide me with a lot more than just the basic necessities.

Also, the level of difficulty that had to be overcome to locate my file had opened my eyes to the immediate need to convert the hard-copy documents into a digital format so that they could be preserved and easily accessible. If not, then it would only be a matter of time before such vital information was no longer available to the thousands of children who had passed through the CDA.

Throughout one of my conversations with Mrs. Riley and Ms. Clarke, they highlighted one critical area of need, which had to do with assisting children who were in the process of transitioning from the care and supervision of the CDA to be on their own. Not every child who found him- or herself in the care of the CDA would be fortunate enough to be adopted, fostered, or placed in the care of a family member. Therefore, after reaching the age of eighteen, such a child would be left to fend for him- or herself. Although the first fifteen years of my life were plagued with many physical and psychological misfortunes, I was very fortunate that, in the end, God provided a compassionate person, Aunt Lucy, who was there for me every step of the way. Therefore, on my eighteenth birthday, I did not have to worry about where I would go and to whom. Neither did I have to worry about my essential needs. Unfortunately, this was not the same regarding my only brother.

This trip also reinforced the point that, over the years, I have survived not of my own accord, but by the grace of God, who has allowed me to overcome what was once perceived as "impossible odds." Finally, after reading through many years' worth of information concerning my brother and me, and after inquiring about the policies and procedures of the CDA, I boarded a flight and returned to the United States of America.

**Back to the Future**

Once again, I found myself driving all over South Florida, but still was unable to find a full-time job. I remember trying to figure out why I was being rejected by the companies I interviewed with even though I was quite optimistic after the process. I even went as far as to adopt different interviewing techniques. Not only that, but I gave my car a professional paint job because I thought that I was being rejected because my car was old, banged up, and rusty. Well, I was the one who sort of messed up the appearance of the car when I tried to do the paint job myself but only made matters worse. See for yourself.

Note to self, and to everyone as well, please do not try to paint your vehicle with aerosol-can spray paint that you have purchased at your local hardware store.

## Chapter 15

As you can see, the little donkey has taken a beating and kept on going and going.

Regardless of my relentless job search and the many corrective measures I adopted, the year 2009 went by and I was still without a full-time job. To complicate the matter, I was not entitled to any unemployment benefits. Although the United States provides a tremendous amount of opportunities, I realized that for me to provide for my family, I need to revisit my Jamaican survival experiences. With that said, I decided that the 2010 calendar year was all about trusting in God and going wherever opportunity led. After discussing my bold new initiative with my wife, I decided to spread my wings far beyond Florida and expand my job search to all of the United States, including Guam. Technically, I did not include Guam, but next time I might because when a man is desperate for work, there will be no uncharted territory. Finally, after several weeks of my nationwide search, I was contacted by two recruiters, Michelle and Laura, from Apex System, Charlotte, North Carolina. I was informed of two job opportunities located in the financial district of Charlotte. However, I was told

## The Journey

that I had to attend an in-person interview for both jobs at my own expense.

According to Google Maps, a trip from Florida to North Carolina should have been an easy drive. Or in the words of a Jamaican, "A nuh far man; a just roun a di cana!" ("It is not too far away; it is just around the corner.") Now that all roads were leading to North Carolina, it was time for me to take a ride with opportunity. However, I learned rather quickly that it was much easier said than done. After the first 200 miles, I started questioning my wisdom regarding driving some 640 miles in a beat-up 1999 Nissan Sentra with approximately 200,000 miles. Besides, I was going against conventional wisdom because if it had proven impossible for me to find a job within a 200-mile radius, then what would make me believe that a 600-mile trip would be any different? Although it is not possible to predict in a quantifiable way the magnitude of one's determination, nonetheless, I knew that I had enough faith to justify the need for this trip. So, after a long, twelve-hour journey, I finally made it to North Carolina!

I booked into a Days Inn motel that was located within a couple of blocks of the interview site. I was hoping for a good night's rest but, unfortunately, that did not happen because the heater broke. After several hours of unsuccessful attempts, the maintenance person gave up and told me that I should request to be transferred to another room. It was 3:00 a.m. and I was in no mood for a transfer. Although it was quite cold inside the room, I told him that I would stay put. The minute I dozed off, my wake-up alarm rang. I could barely get out of bed because my entire body was aching. To compound the matter, the minute I was about to step through the door, the rain came pouring down. It

## Chapter 15

was raining as though the skies had opened up right over the motel. I was very fortunate that Michelle and Laura (Apex Systems recruiters) came by and provided me with a ride to the interview. If I had not gotten a ride, I would certainly have found myself taking another shower on my way to the interview. However, it turned out that the downpour was the least of my problems. That morning, we kept running from one place to the next only to discover that we were in the wrong building. After running among several buildings for approximately thirty-five minutes, we finally located the correct one. And guess what? The irony was that the building was not even a Bank of America center. The interview was being conducted in the Branch Banking and Trust (BB&T) building, which is another banking center.

What a conundrum! Nonetheless, I needed to get to the interview as soon as possible because I was already thirty minutes late. With that said, I ran into the building and took one of the elevators to the twelfth floor. The minute I got out of the elevator, I was greeted by Subburaj, the interviewer. I thought he was there to let me know that he had canceled the interview but, to my surprise, that was not the case. Instead, he greeted me with a pleasant good morning and escorted me into one of the conference rooms.

Now that everything was in place, it was time for us to get going with the long-awaited interview. Well, not so fast. If you think that arriving at an interview late was all I had to contend with, then think again. The minute I sat down, my mind went off into a faraway déjà vu land. I do recall hearing Subburaj speaking, but for some unknown reason, I was unable to comprehend any of what he was

*The Journey*

saying. The long drive, the lack of sleep, and the constant running around to the different buildings had drained every joule of energy I had. I had no brainpower to provide him the answer to his questions. However, Subburaj detected that something was wrong. He asked, "What is the matter? Is something wrong?" That was when I gathered myself and told him about the long and gruesome drive from Florida, my lack of sleep due to a broken heater at the motel, and the exhaustive runaround I had performed just to find the correct building. At that moment, I thought the interview was over and he was about to escort me to the door. However, what transpired next was something that reminded me that patience is indeed a reflection of virtue. Instead of escorting me to the door, he provided me with some time so that I could relax. Lord knows I needed that little break. I was delighted to have a couple of minutes to catch my breath and reenergize my brain cells. Well, it was my fault for not staying at the Holiday Inn Express instead of a Days Inn. Okay, the above statement is not something for you to think about. I am merely using an old but clever Holiday Inn Express advertisement to poke a little fun at my not-so-pleasant situation.

After Subburaj was through with the first section of the interview, he allowed me to take another twenty-to thirty-minute break before proceeding to the next phase of the interview. At the end of the interview, I was offered a six-month contract with the Bank of America Corporation. I was very happy! It made the 640-mile journey a worthwhile effort. It was a joy to know that after incurring a little over four hundred dollars' debt on a credit card and spending many hours driving to North Carolina, I was finally going home with a great reward. Now that I

## Chapter 15

had gotten over the interview process and had received a six-month contract, all I had to do was to sit back, relax, and wait for the recruiter to finalize my start date with Bank of America.

**Intervention**

While I was at home, waiting patiently, at 9:07 a.m. on March 3, 2010, I received an email from Facebook. The minute I opened the email, I noticed that the message was from Carol Johnson. Her message was as follows, "Oh my God! Is this Desmond who I used to board with at . . . ?" She was referring to my former foster parents, whose names I have omitted. When I saw her message, I was overwhelmed with joy because I knew right away that Carol was indeed one of the Johnsons who had boarded with my former foster parents. If you need a refresher on the Johnsons, please review volume 2 of my autobiography. This was the first time I had heard from her since her mother removed her and her siblings from my former foster parents' home. It had been approximately thirty years, so I had no idea if I would ever see or hear from them again. However, that yearning desire was put to rest when I got the above message from Carol.

With this much excitement in the air, we could not resist catching up on old times. With that said, I contacted Carol, and she went ahead and established a conference call with her siblings, Ann and Maxwell. We talked for almost two hours, mostly reminiscing on the days we had spent with my former foster parents. We tried to poke a little fun at some of my foster parent's actions. Unfortunately, even the ones we considered to be mild brought

*The Journey*

back many dark and painful memories. This was especially true for the ones concerning my only brother. However, the one takeaway that resonates in my mind to this very day was when they told me that for over thirty years, their hearts had gone out to my brother and me because of the inhumane treatment we were subjected to at the hands of our foster parents, more so our foster mother. The Johnsons were not the only ones who had been concerned about our well-being. In fact, a number of our peers who were aware of the environment that we were subjected to would also voice similar concerns. One of their most notable concerns was that of my brother. On several occasions, they would remind me how emotionally distraught my brother had become as a result of our foster parents' unjust treatment. Sometimes they would follow up by saying, "Desmond! We don't know how you lived under such brutal conditions and turned out the way you are." Although I was not fully aware then, today I know with all certainty that it was God who helped me to cope throughout such times. I also believe that my sense of humor eased the psychological pain I felt deep within my soul. Throughout such times, and even to this very day, my desire is always to see smiles and to hear laughter.

I must admit that those memories brought back lingering psychological pain, especially when I think of my brother and the other children who were subjected to my former foster parents' inhumane treatment. However, I was very fortunate to have had a wonderful foster mother who brought joy and happiness to my life, especially throughout my adolescent years. In addition to my foster mother, there were many other people whom I have highlighted throughout the writing of my autobiography.

## Chapter 15

These individuals have stood by me and have become mentors and parents to me. Unfortunately, I am unable to say the same concerning my only brother. He did not have someone to love and care for him, especially throughout his adolescent years, which became the primary reason for his downfall. One of the pressing questions I pondered over quite often is this: Could it be that my former foster parents believed in their hearts that the manner in which they treated the children, more so the foster children, was justified? Could it be that they were so entrenched in their selfish desires that they could not have known that their actions were causing physical and psychological harm to the very children they were entrusted to care for? I sincerely hope that they came to terms with their actions and sought forgiveness in such regard.

**Perception**

After a month of waiting impatiently, I finally commenced my six-month contract with the Bank of America Corporation (BOA) located in Charlotte, North Carolina. I was very excited and, with no hesitation, on March 21, 2010, I saddled up "The Little Donkey" and galloped all the way from Florida to North Carolina. Well, that statement is a bit misleading, so here is the revised version. After receiving the good news, I bid goodbye to my family, filled the gas tank of my Nissan Sentra, and drove 640 miles back to North Carolina to start my long-awaited contract with Bank of America. By the way, I refer to the Nissan Sentra as "The Little Donkey" because even when I had it packed from floor to roof with all sorts of bangarang, it never quit. Used and abused, it kept chugging along. Anyway, now

## The Journey

that I was back in North Carolina, I needed a place to stay for the interim. And guess what? I had not learned my lesson from my first experience because I decided to stay at the same Days Inn motel for a second time. The Days Inn motel turned out to be the most economical choice because I was scheduled to be in North Carolina for the first week of the contract and then work from home in Florida for the remaining five months and three weeks. I officially started my contract with BOA on March 22, 2010.

The first week was dedicated to orientation and getting the necessary resources (laptop, access privileges, etc.) squared away. Subburaj, my manager, assisted me with the onboarding process and other intricacies that are associated with the job. Before I knew it, Monday through Thursday went by rather quickly. Although it was only a six-month contract, it was still a joy to know that after enduring many rejections for over a year, I had finally received a full-time job. However, somewhere around 4:30 p.m. on Friday, March 26, 2010, I received a call on my cell phone. Usually, I do not answer my cell phone while in the office, but seeing that it was from Apex Systems (my recruiter), then it was a call worth taking. The minute I answered the phone, the person told me that I should go by the Caribou Coffee on the third floor of the BB&T building and one of the company's representatives would meet me there. I tried to inquire about the reason, but she would not provide me with the reason. Instead, she replied, "Please meet the representative at the Caribou Coffee shop now!" Although the conversation ended abruptly, I needed to find a way to generate positive thoughts so, I started singing Bob Marley's, "Don't worry about a thing, 'cause every little thing gonna be all right" song. Well, I must confess that I way too worried

## Chapter 15

about the outcome, but if I had thought about singing, then that would definitely have been my choice song.

Seeing that I would be working from home for the remainder of the six-month contract (well, that was what I thought), I took some time and packed away all my belongings, including the Bank's laptop. After I was through, I took the elevator to the third floor and hurried over to Caribou Coffee. Although I do not drink coffee, in this context, it would not be a bad idea for me to discuss my current and future job opportunities over a cup of afternoon coffee. However, as soon as I made eye contact with the Apex Systems representative, I noticed that he was not looking too happy. Without any hesitation, he told me that Bank of America did not need my services anymore and that today would be my last day on the job.

At first, I thought he was pulling a fast one on me or, as we would say in Jamaica, "A joke im a joke, man!" Just to confirm, I asked, "You mean this is it for the six-month contract?"

He replied, "Yes, according to the bank." Then he asked me to turn over to him everything I had in my possession that belonged to Bank of America.

Ladies and gentlemen, that was when it dawned on me that this was the end of the employment road for me. With so much disappointment, one would have thought that the recruiter would at least have soothed my wounds by handing me my week's pay. No sir! That was only wishful thinking on my part because that did not happen. Instead, he bid me good luck and goodbye. Good luck and goodbye were the last words I heard from the Apex Systems representative before he left me standing in the middle of nowhere. Come to think of it, he did not even offer me a cup of coffee.

After the work drama was over, I went to Maxwell's home to catch up on old times. As I alluded to earlier, Maxwell is one of the Johnsons (Carol and Ann's brother) who had been boarding at my former foster parents' home. He was now residing in Charlotte, North Carolina, and his home was within proximity to the corporate center. After not seeing him for approximately thirty years, I decided to use this opportunity to visit him before heading back to Florida. I was very fortunate to have a friend close by because this was one of the times when misery needed a lot of company. Not only was I going to Maxwell's home to celebrate our long-awaited reunion, but I was also there to break the bad news to him that the six-month contract had been pulled right out from beneath me. It was like catching a huge fish at the end of a lousy fishing day only to witness it jump right out of my hands and back into the water.

Despite the lost opportunity, I had a wonderful time with Maxwell and his family. That day I slept over because I was too tired and way too disappointed to embark on a twelve-hour, 640-mile drive back to Florida. The following morning, Saturday, before I set out on my long journey, Maxwell shared a word of prayer, followed by the reading of Psalm 37: 25, ESV. He quoted David, "I have been young, and now am old, yet I have not seen the righteous forsaken or his children begging for bread." Well, that is indeed a testament to my life, because even throughout the desperate times I spent with my mother as a child, I was privileged to have received a little piece of bread when possible. In addition to the uplifting and encouraging words, Maxwell also financed my fuel cost back to Florida. Although the

## Chapter 15

job had ended prematurely, I did not regret my trip because I had an opportunity to reunite with my friend after thirty years. Besides, this opportunity paved the way for my next job. When it was all over, on Saturday, March 27, 2010, I commenced my long 640-mile journey back to Florida.

After spending over nine hundred dollars on a credit card for a job that had lasted only one week, the real dilemma was how to break the disappointing news to my family. Instead of waiting until I got home, I decided to break the news to them while I was on my way. I did so just in case they planned on greeting me with "an exquisite robe and a fatted calf" (a biblical reference). With my full-time job now gone with the wind, it was time to go back to the drawing board to see what other opportunities were beyond the horizon. At least North Carolina had given me a lot more than Florida because I had been offered a job and even allowed to work for a week.

**The Relentless Pursuit**

It appeared as though I were destined to work out of Charlotte because after spending approximately two months at home and not receiving any job offers, I was once again contacted by Michelle, from Apex Systems. Surprisingly enough, the call was in regard to another contract with Bank of America. I remember she asked if I were interested and with no hesitation whatever I said, "Sure!" I guess she thought that I would decline the offer based on my most recent experience with Bank of America. Well, let's look on the bright side; if a six-month contract lasted for five days, then there was a strong probability that a three-month contract would last at least two days. After I was through with the interviews via the phone (this time, I did not have to drive 640 miles to North Carolina), an offer was extended unto me by John Barger, which I accepted graciously. This time, I was scheduled to work exclusively out of the office located in Charlotte, North Carolina, and not from my home like the first contract. This opportunity was causing me to be away from my family for the duration. Not only that, but I also had a twelve-hour commute to get home on the weekends. This opportunity would cause me to be away from my family for the duration. Not only that, but I also would have a twenty-four-hour commute to and from North Carolina on the weekends and holidays I visit home. Nonetheless, I was desperate, and having a little money to pay the bills was worth the effort.

After arranging my living accommodations, I packed my Nissan Sentra from floor to roof with all the necessities. Later that afternoon, I bid a happy-sad goodbye to my wife and daughter before commencing yet another 640-mile journey back to Charlotte. On May 17, 2010, I started my second contract with Bank of America. I was assigned to work out of the same BB&T building. However, this time around, I was assigned to the eleventh floor instead of the twelfth floor. My reaction was that if Bank of America continued with this "dandy shandy" hiring practice, then I would certainly have ten more floors to go before the company could finally have a reason to get rid of me for good.

## Life in All Its Glory

On June 17, 2010, while I was on the job toiling away, trying to bring the family financial ends within reach, my wife gave me surprising but exciting news. She told me that

## Chapter 15

we were expecting our second child. For a brief moment, I was left speechless. She asked, "Are you excited?"

To which I replied, "Sure, I am!" Due to my work schedule, our conversation was cut short. At that defining moment, a million thoughts were flowing through my mind. I was so overwhelmed that I completely forgot everything that I was supposed to be doing that afternoon. However, I was quickly brought back to reality when I realized that the financial ends that I was trying desperately to amend had just gotten a lot further apart. Regardless of my financial struggles, my joy was magnified because I no longer had that overwhelming fear of my childhood reminding me that I was not capable of being a loving and caring father.

## CHAPTER 16

# REUNITING WITH MY ONLY BROTHER

Finally, after having had no contact with my brother, George, for approximately fifteen years, on November 10, 2010, I had an opportunity to be reunited with him. This outcome was indeed a divine intervention because it turned out to be our last and final reunion. It happened while I was visiting with Inez in Montego Bay. My nephew came inside the house and told me that my brother was outside and asked if I would like to speak with him. One would wonder why my nephew had to ask my permission instead of just inviting my brother (his uncle) inside so that we could enjoy a well overdue brotherly relationship.

Although it is not easy for me to put in words, I will try to do so regardless. The previous contacts I had with my brother had left me with painful memories of what had become of him. The brother I grew up with, the brother who was there for me, the brother who once had the mental and intellectual capacity to become a proud and resourceful member of society, was now considered and treated as society's outcast. Every time that I would inquire of my brother, I was always provided with gruesome depictions concerning his physical and psychological being. These depictions

## Chapter 16

linger in my mind to this very day and have left me with a grieving soul. I was deeply troubled, knowing that I did not have the financial means to help him. For these reasons, I had not made a concerted effort to see him. I was hoping that the next time we met, I would be able to remove him from the streets and place him in an institution where his medical, physical, and psychological needs would be met.

Before compiling my life story, and not having a full understanding of why my brother had ventured down the dark and lonely path of drugs and alcohol, I was always asking myself why George had resorted to such destructive measures. Why had he complicated his life with drugs and alcohol? Why? Why? And why? However, instead of being so judgmental toward my brother, I should have realized that he was never given the same opportunities I was fortunate to have received. He never had a foster mother like Aunt Lucy to love and care for him. Instead of being so critical of my brother, I should have asked myself these two fundamental questions. First, how could my brother have known the correct path and the appropriate actions to take when the very people who had been entrusted to care for his physical, emotional, social, and psychological needs had completely neglected their responsibilities? Second, what opportunity or set of opportunities were made available to my brother when our foster parents took him to a juvenile correctional institution that made it virtually impossible for him to experience a life filled with hope, dreams, and aspirations? Now I understand what my brother meant when he told me that he had chosen this path (drugs and alcohol) as a way to ease the pain. Now I realize that my brother was not trying to address the physical pain but, instead, the psychological pain.

However, my traumatic experience with Company Zen provided me with a glimpse into the dark chapters of my brother's childhood psychological struggles. This experience made me realize that this day was different and that now was the most appropriate time to speak with my brother. No matter what condition my brother was in, he was and would always be my only brother. Moreover, my emotional pain was quite minuscule when compared to the physical and psychological suffering my brother had to endure each and every day of his life. With such an overwhelming conviction of the heart, I went outside to see him, to speak with him, and to find out what was going on in his life.

Once again, I could clearly see that this person was not the brother I once knew. Nevertheless, the "eternal" silence was broken when I heard my brother say, "Look mi bredda! A mi spirit tell mi yuh deh-yah." ("Look! Here is my brother! My spirit told me that you are here.") After we greeted each other, he showed me several bumps and bruises on his forehead, including a busted lip. He told me that he had been beaten up by two guys while he was on his way to our sister's home. Not only had they physically abused him, but they had also robbed him of the little money he had. Throughout our conversation, I asked him why he had decided to come to our sister's home. He told me that he had stopped by for a piece of bread to go along with a small tin of sardines he was holding in his hand. I inquired of him how he had come by the tin of sardines, and he said that he had bought it with the money he had earned by cleaning the debris from one of the residents' roofs.

While my brother and I were at the gate talking, two young men came by to inquire if he (my brother) was causing trouble or being a nuisance to the family. My brother

## Chapter 16

was speaking in a rather loud manner, which prompted one of the guys to ask, "A wah a gwan? A dis yah madman yah a gi unnu trouble?" ("What is going on here? Is this madman or insane person causing trouble?") George was quite upset with the young man for addressing him in such a manner. Immediately, I intervened and told them that he was my brother and was not causing any trouble but, instead, was quite happy to see me. To affirm, one of the young men said to me, "A Woka Man a yuh breda?" ("Is Woka Man [Worker Man] your brother?") I replied that he was indeed my brother. I followed up by asking the man why he had addressed my brother as Woka Man and, with no hesitation whatsoever, he replied, "No man pan de face a de earth can wok like disyah man." ("There is no other person on the face of the earth can work like this man.") What he was saying was that, to his knowledge, my brother's work ethic was unmatched by any other person. Although I am not able to go as far as to say that my brother was the most dedicated worker in the world, upon hearing such a profound statement, I knew right away that this assertion was not a fabricated one, nor was it a lightly made-up gesture. Several people told me that my brother was the most dedicated worker of the Catherine Hall housing complex, where he resided.

As a matter of fact, on several occasions when I inquired of my brother, my nephew told me that he had seen him going to and from the Catherine Hall housing complex with a large container on his head filled with debris. Although my brother was considered a squatter and a madman, he worked tirelessly and relentlessly day after day doing many of the residents' manual chores. His daily tasks included using a machete to chop and groom trees, shrubs, lawns, and gardens. After he was through, he would remove the debris from their yards and surrounding areas. He also picked fruit, and ran errands and performed just about any other manual chores that needed to be done. His work ethic explained why everyone in the Catherine Hall housing complex and neighboring districts addressed him as Woka Man.

Concerning my brother's being labeled a very hard worker, that is a trait I have personally witnessed and one that I can attest to. This assertion was nothing out of the ordinary because while living with our foster parents, my brother was the chief architect with regard to the farm duties and most of the yard chores. His daily tasks included taking care of the animals; chopping (with a machete) and removing the grass and shrubs from the lawn, flower gardens, and surrounding areas; building and repairing the chicken coops and pigpens; gathering firewood from the nearby bushes that were needed to boil many containers of water to facilitate the cleaning of the chickens and the animal carcasses; slaughtering chickens; and cleaning the carcasses and organs after the butchers were through slaughtering the animals. My brother also built the handcart that we used to transport the building materials, dried wood (used as a source of fuel), and animal feed to and from the different the home and farms. Many mornings before I was awake, my brother was already up before daylight initiating the process needed to take care of the chores, including the chickens and the other farm animals.

In addition to my brother's work ethic, I was also told by several of his acquaintances that he was quite intelligent. Although my brother attended school for only three and a half years, I was told that throughout the brief moments

## Chapter 16

that he was in his right frame of mind, his reasoning and intellectual abilities surpassed those of a college graduate. As it pertained to his reasoning and intellectual abilities, that was also true because he would put forth constructive reasoning to our foster parents concerning their injustice.

Although I did not want to rehash the abuse we had endured while living with our foster parents, I did so merely to uncover if my brother's psychological effects were similar to what I experienced while working at Company Zen. That is, I needed to find out if the unjust treatment that he had endured while living with our foster parents was the cause of his psychological pain. Despite his obscure frame of mind, my brother remembered quite well and was deeply troubled. At one point throughout our conversation, he fell to the ground and wept. With tears flowing down his cheeks, he said, "Mi a weh de bad bwoy, an yuh a weh di good bwoy." ("I was the bad boy, and you were the good boy.") Then he pleaded with me, "Mi bredda, help mi fi come back to miself." ("My brother, please help me to come back to myself.") It was quite painful for me to continue, so I changed the conversation to a lighter subject. It was at that defining moment that I witnessed my brother's emotional well-being reflecting not just the physical pain, but the effects of the psychological trauma that had been inflicted upon him by our foster parents.

With such a vivid revelation, I was able to understand why the children who were aware of our traumatic situation had been so concerned about our well-being. This was even more evident with the Johnsons, because they were boarding with our foster parents for a short while. What I had not been aware of at the time was how much they were disturbed by the abuse that was taking place, and the fact that my foster mother was using derogatory terms when addressing the foster children.

This came to light many years later when Maxwell told me that one day, just as the family was seated at the table and was about to eat their meals, a lady who was visiting the family asked my foster mother why my brother and I were not allowed to join the family at the table. With no hesitation whatsoever, she replied, "They are like dogs and are not allowed at the table." Maxwell went on to say that this came as a shock to him and his siblings because they could not believe for a moment that my foster mother would respond in such a manner. This must have been a very frightening experience for this lady too. However, this was the time that this lady, who bore the title of a Christian missionary, should have stood up and corrected my foster mother. Instead, she chose not to. As a matter of fact, all of the adults, including my foster father, should have intervened and let my foster mother know that it was not moral, ethical, or humane for anyone to address children as dogs. However, I was not alarmed by what Maxwell had said because my brother and I were constantly being addressed as dogs and scavengers.

Although it was quite painful for me to accept the premise that my former foster mother meant it literally when she used those derogatory terms to address my brother and me, this was sufficient evidence to remind me that she had, indeed, viewed us as less than a person and not worthy of being treated as human beings. With such a profound recollection, it is quite clear that my brother's soul was burdened with the weight of our foster parents' condemnation of him. It appeared as though my brother had lived his entire life not realizing that he was never a

## Chapter 16

bad or evil person as his foster parents had claimed. Neither was he a dog or a scavenger but, instead, a human being who was only trying to communicate a sense of fairness to our foster parents, more so our foster mother. Moreover, choosing to remain quiet had not made me a good or a better person. It was the mercy of God that had helped me to live in the same environment and maintain my sanity. Only God could have shielded me from much of the psychological pain that had consumed my brother.

Moreover, if my foster parents were correct in their assertion that my brother was an evil person, then such behavior would have manifested itself throughout the times we lived with our father and mother, and, most certainly, throughout the times we spent at the orphanage. I never witnessed my father, mother, or any of the staff members from the orphanage had to take any disciplinary measures against my brother. Therefore, after a thorough examination, I could not find any evidence to substantiate my foster parents' fabricated assertions concerning my brother.

Although my brother never caused any trouble, our foster parents regarded him as a bad person simply because of his relentless pursuit of justice. I chose not to respond verbally to my foster parents', more so my foster mother's, insults and inhumane treatment because I was quite fearful of them and was more concerned with not doing anything that would jeopardize our stay or cause us to lose the little (food and shelter) that we were being offered. However, such a premise did not last, because the very day I spoke out against my foster parents' injustice was the very day I ended up losing the things I had tried to preserve, even at the expense of my only brother. I also found out that my foster parents were never people that we, the foster children, could reason with or participate in any form of rational conversation with.

Today, I realize that I should have stood up with my brother and spoken out against our foster parents' gross injustice, irrespective of the cost. However, the real question that needs to be asked of us today is this: When faced with gross injustice, should we shrink from our responsibilities merely to save ourselves from being criticized and to retain the friendship of those who condone injustice? Knowing what I know now, I would like to say that advocating for justice is a nobler cause than friendship, material possessions, and feckless accolades. I am here to say that the basic principles that are associated with human dignity should never be compromised!

I am not sure what my brother meant when he asked me to bring him back to himself. My brother's request was beyond the scope of my understanding because, throughout his entire life, he was never fortunate to have experienced a normal life. Therefore, it caused me to wonder what point in his past he would like to have been brought back to. Nonetheless, I promised my brother that I would do everything possible to remove him from the streets. My priority was to find him a place where his physical and psychological needs would be met. I would like to stress the psychological needs, because Inez had taken him in and tried to help him, but he did not stay. Aunt Lucy also had pleaded with him but, unfortunately, my brother could not be persuaded. I believe that my brother's mental condition prevented him from distinguishing between those who were genuinely trying to help him and those who meant him harm.

My brother was at the point in his life where he was no longer capable of making rational decisions. Based on his

## Chapter 16

plea, I knew that he had become emotionally distraught. However, the most painful outcome for me was the fact that my brother seemed to have known that his life was in the wrong place but was unable to do anything about it. Prior to this experience, all I could hear was my brother's outward cry. Unfortunately, his emotional plea for help had become an echo that only he could hear. It is quite painful to know that my brother had to roam the streets with no future and, most of all, no hope. My brother's life was further complicated because no one understood his childhood physical and psychological struggles. And because of that, society labeled him an insane person and treated him with much disdain.

One of the most chilling and frightening incidents concerning my brother, was related to me by Inez. George had been in the hospital due to severe burns that he had suffered to most of his body. Apparently, there were several assertions relating to this incident, nonetheless, the outcome remains the same. My brother was doused with Jamaican overproof rum and set on fire because someone wanted to get rid of him. In some instances, the family would describe his condition to me in very graphic terms such as rotten flesh and stinky body odor, as a result of his many open wounds.

These incidents brought tears to my eyes, especially when I remember the day that I had stood there and watched as my former foster parents took my brother away from me and dropped him off at the worst juvenile correctional institution, Copse Place of Safety for boys. Not because he deserved it! Not because he was a bad person! Not because he had violated any laws! But simply because he was asking for basic fairness and refused to accept the unacceptable. My brother was only asking for the things

## Reuniting With My Only Brother

that any fair-minded person would provide freely unto his or her own child. Instead, he was forced to live in deplorable conditions amongst other juveniles, several of whom had violated the law in many respects. This incident brought me to tears many times, especially throughout the writing of the dark and lonely chapters of his life.

I also remember the day my brother visited me while I was living with Aunt Lucy, and how he had tried to convince me to leave the Babylonian way of life and return to our father's home in Zion. The most painful outcome of that reunion was the fact that we, Aunt Lucy and I, had been unable to persuade him otherwise. At that point, my brother had long given up on everyone and everything except our father's Rastafarian ideology.

I was always looking forward to the day when my brother was no longer on the streets. A day when he would no longer have to worry about his basic needs. A day when his basic dignity and self-worth could be elevated to that of a human being. A day when we would have the opportunity to sit down and share brotherly conversations that were filled with moments of laughter and friendly gestures. A day when I would let him know that I cared deeply about his well-being. Unfortunately, that day was much easier to conceive than it was to bring to fruition.

My brother's needs were far more pressing than just food, clothes, and shelter. I struggled with the possibility of knowing that, for me to help my brother, I would have no other choice but to remove him from the streets and place him in an institution where his freedom would be greatly restricted. Such a decision raised two fundamental questions. First, what if removing George from the streets and placing him in solitary confinement, with the best of

## Chapter 16

intentions, ended up causing him to suffer greater psychological harm? Second, would my brother have known that I was doing this because I cared deeply about his well-being, or would he have viewed it otherwise? With these pressing concerns at the forefront of my mind, I was deeply torn, trying to come up with the right set of actions to take on George's behalf. I can assure you that, although it would have been vital to his recovery, the isolation and restriction measures troubled me greatly.

Moreover, the isolation and restriction measures were precisely what our foster parents had resorted to when they took him to the juvenile correctional institution. Their actions negated the possibility of my brother's pursuing a normal life. At one point, I found myself contemplating the idea of letting George know that for me to bring him back to himself, he would have to be placed in an institution that would limit his freedom. However, despite my good intentions, that premise would have been a lie because I knew full well that it was impossible for me to bring him back to himself, not knowing to which self or to what point in his past he was referring to. In the end, I was heartbroken, knowing that I was leaving my brother in such a deplorable state.

This outcome is a staunch reminder to us parents (biological, adopted, foster, or legal guardian) that there are tremendous consequences when we neglect our responsibilities with regard to the well-being of our children or the children who have been placed in our care. Today, the only difference between my brother and me is the fact that I was given a second chance for life and the pursuit of happiness. Had it not been for the grace of God, and for wonderful and responsible individuals such as Aunt Lucy, I would not have realized that my life had any value. While living with my former foster parents, I really thought that the only value a child living in an orphanage had was to become someone's servant, maid, or domestic helper. I could only wonder what my brother's life would have been had he not been deprived of his human dignity and had been allowed to realize his dreams.

In retrospect, I felt as though I had abandoned my only brother. I felt as though I had not made the necessary effort to be there for him when he needed a brother. There were times when I would try to convince my brother that it was ok to be addressed as dogs and scavengers because, from my perspective, psychological abuse was a lighter form of punishment when compared to the physical abuse we had to endure. Sometimes I had found myself thinking that by being too outspoken, my brother would cause us to lose everything. There were times when I had tried to convince my brother that it was in our interest to conform to our foster parents' injustice.

However, today, I find myself wondering if the outcome of my brother's life would have been different had I joined in solidarity with him and spoken out against our foster parents' injustice, irrespective of the costs. In retrospect, I should have joined in solidarity with my brother when he told our foster parents that he would not take care of the farm and the animals unless we were treated as human beings. However, throughout such times, I continued with the farm chores, thus undermining my brother's effort. I should have joined with my brother throughout the times he was denied his meals.

Many times, I found myself wondering what the outcome would have been if all the children in the home had

## Chapter 16

stood up and, in a collective manner, refused our meals as well. That way, we would have sent a clear and collective message to our foster parents and legal guardians by letting them know that if a child has been denied his basic needs, then all of the children in the home have been denied their basic needs. If a child has been being addressed as a dog and scavenger, then all of the children in the home have also been addressed as dogs and scavengers.

Today, I am left wondering if the outcome would have been different if I had been there with my brother the day our foster parents returned him to the Child Development Agency (CDA). That way, we could have brought to the agency's attention the abuse that was taking place at home. Instead of being a loyal supporter, I chose to save myself from further physical abuse and to safeguard the little life-sustaining benefits that our foster parents were providing us. I did so, even at the expense of my own only brother! By not being there with my brother at such a critical juncture, I most likely give the CDA representatives the impression that I was a good boy and my brother a bad boy. Why did I not see the injustice that my brother had seen? Why had I not taken an active role in fighting against the injustice that my brother fought against unyieldingly? Why did I not join in solidarity with my brother and support his cause? I do understand that fear and intimidation caused me not to confront our foster parents the way my brother did. Nonetheless, today, I am left wondering if the outcome would have been different had I stood in solidarity with my brother and challenged our foster parent's injustice.

One of the first steps in destroying George's life was through baseless accusations. Our foster parents assign unto him labels such as dog, vulture, scavenger, ill-mannered, bad, evil, and more, which would then be used as justification for their abusive actions. Second, they tried to convince everyone that because my brother had been assigned those labels, then he should be punished, isolated, and deprived of his basic life-sustaining needs.

Some might suggest that my brother was overly sensitive or too emotional, thus the reason for much of his psychological pain. Some might even go as far as to say that my brother was ungrateful and did not appreciate the fact that his foster parents had rescued him from an orphanage and provided him with the basic necessities, such as a home, food, and clothes. However, after compiling our life's story, I am entirely convinced that my brother's mental suffering was not caused by his personality. Instead, it had everything to do with George being shunned, humiliated, and addressed as a dog and scavenger. Being denied his meals and being forced to work in maggot-filled pigpens and chicken coops without the proper working attire, not even a pair of shoes to protect his feet. Being physically and psychologically abused because he stood up for justice. Being told that he would never come to anything good in life. Being told that he would live and die like a dog. Being told that if he did not appreciate how he was being treated, then he was free to leave (or, in our foster mother's words, "He is free to go back where he came from"). Being separated from his family, including his only brother. And finally, being taken to one of the worst juvenile institutions. If these are not reasons for a child to have a cynical view of the world, including his oppressors, then I am not sure what else would! This is a reminder for all of us that if we are ignorant of the facts, then we are definitely not in a position to judge.

## Chapter 16

In the end, my brother did not prevail in his relentless pursuit of justice. His voice and his actions were not conclusive enough to change the hearts and minds of his oppressors. And because of that, today, my reminiscing of my only brother has undoubtedly become my most painful lamentation. It is a constant reminder that injustice is not something that can easily be forgotten. Injustice does not fade away over time, nor can it be swept under a rug. Instead, injustice is a wrong that must be rectified through just actions, irrespective of the costs. Today, I believe that my brother's consciousness regarding injustice was a divine intervention and one that needs to be echoed throughout the entire world.

I am quite heartbroken and emotionally distraught to see what had become of my only brother (2010).

The person on the right is the brother I once knew. (1979).

# CHAPTER 17

# HOME SWEET HOME

Seeing that we were looking forward to the birth of our second child, I was faced with yet another important decision regarding my family. Living and working in North Carolina was not the ideal situation, especially at such a crucial time. On the one hand, I was very grateful for my job and would do everything possible to keep it. On the other hand, I knew how important it was for me to be home with my family. After much consideration, I decided to discuss the situation with my manager, John. to my surprise, he did not turn me away. Instead, he provided me with the opportunity to enroll in the Bank of America work-from-home program.

Wow! This opportunity was yet another undeserved blessing that had exceeded my wildest imagination! There I was, thinking that I would have to say goodbye to my job, but instead, I was allowed to be home with my family and keep my job too. Have you heard the saying, "Never take the job home with you"? In this instance, I was more than happy to take my job home with me. Being able to work from home and to be with my family was a new year's resolution I could only have dreamt about. Not only that, but as time progressed, I came to realize that one of the most

# Chapter 17

important values of the work-from-home program was the fact that it provided me with uninterrupted devotional time with my Lord. This outcome was one more reason why I will never cease to be grateful to God for all my blessings.

Just when I thought that everything was smooth sailing, a little sorrow snuck in and dampened my going-home joy. Just before I said goodbye to North Carolina, I came down with a severe skin disorder. I mean, one day I was fine, the next day my entire body was covered with an unexplainable rash. I thought this illness would last only for a couple of days, but I was wrong. In fact, my illness turned out to be an eleven-month ordeal. However, the work-from-home option made it possible for me to continue working despite my illness. Once again, I was reminded of the "no pain, no gain" philosophy. Also, this was another shipment of young mangoes from my dream, the ones that signify hardship.

Before I proceed to the next segment of my life, I would like to take this opportunity to say a big thank you to my trusted neighbors, "Uncle" Stanley, Mr. P., and Mr. Mercado, for being my emergency contacts while I was away from home. They were always there whenever something at home was broken and needed a man-u-labor intervention. One of the most notable moments was when my wife contacted me and told me that the kitchen faucet was broken and needed immediate attention because the water was gushing all over the place like Dunn's River Falls. Well, she did not mention a word about Dunn's River Falls, but I just wanted to dramatize it a bit. Anyway, I remember contacting Mr. Mercado, and sure enough, he went over immediately and corrected the problem.

I would like to say one more thank you to another special neighbor. In addition to my other illnesses, I also developed a gluten intolerance problem that had plagued me for five years. After many doctor and specialist visits with no success, a significant breakthrough came when my wife told me to contact one of her former coworkers, Scott. Although not a medical doctor, Scott diagnosed my problem and discovered that I was gluten intolerant and needed to go on a gluten-free diet. I can assure you that this information literally saved my life. This is why I would like to take this moment to say a special thank you to Scott for accepting my distress call and diagnosing my problem like a true medical professional.[9]

Although Scott is over a thousand miles away, I also classify him as my neighbor. Moreover, I believe that with today's technological advancements, a neighbor is only a text or a phone call away. So, once again, like good neighbors, they were always there. Hmmm, it sounds like I stole a little of a State Farm advert. Anyway, the point I would like to emphasize is that these acts of kindness further prove why no one person is an island, and no person stands alone! The fact is, my survival depends on your survival.

---

9 I can assure you that sticking to a gluten-free diet is quite challenging. It is like being physically removed from the norms of society. Nonetheless, I have to be disciplined for my own health.

# CHAPTER 18

# THE AFFLICTED

**Envisioning the Unthinkable**

Approximately one year after visiting with my brother, George, I dreamt that something terrible was about to happen to him. Although it was just a dream, it was enough for me to be concerned. With that in mind, I contacted my sister, Inez, and told her that I was quite worried about our brother. I stressed my concern to her by informing her about the dream I had regarding our brother. She assured me that he was okay. To further calm my fears, she told me that he had recently stopped by her home, and she had given him food along with the clothes I had left there. I also spoke with my mother-in-law, Marlene, sharing my dream and the urgent need to remove my brother from the streets. Although I lacked the necessary financial resources to facilitate this endeavor, I did not let that stop me from inquiring about a place that would be suitable for my brother, even if it were temporary.

Six months later, the unthinkable happened when, on June 1, 2012, my sister, Paulette, informed me that George had passed away. She told me that he had fallen from a tree

## Chapter 18

and broken his neck while harvesting fruit for an elderly lady. The day of his burial, I remember standing there, gazing at my brother as he lay in the casket. I could not help but wonder what his life would have been had he not been deprived of his human dignity by the very foster parents who had been entrusted to provide him with the love and care he desperately needed. They degraded him by telling him that he would live and die like a dog. He was physically and psychologically abused for no apparent reason other than speaking out against our foster parents' injustice, more so their hypocrisy and cruelty. My former foster parents' injustice went unchallenged, which in turn prolonged the suffering of the children. They used their superficial wealth and status to influence the majority, including the church and the Child Development Agency. Whenever my brother spoke out against their injustice, they denied him his meals and other basic necessities until he was forced to surrender to their demands. They resorted to this and other extreme coercive measures to send a clear message that no one should dare to challenge their authority.

Out of all the events that took place on that day, the one that resonates with me even now was when I overheard many people addressing my brother as Ainsworth. I remember inquiring about why my brother was being addressed as Ainsworth when his name was George. They told me that my brother had informed them that his name was Ainsworth, not George. That was when it dawned on me that I had lived with my brother his entire childhood and early adolescent years but had never known his name. This is more evidence to prove that from the perspective of others, including me, my brother was and will forever be "The Existence of the Unknown."

## Faced with a Dark Reality

Every time that I reflect on my former foster parents, I wonder why it was acceptable to them to sacrifice the well-being of innocent children just to accumulate more material possessions. How could they display so little regard for the children who were being harmed in the process? It was as if the lives and the well-being of the children were insignificant. Their self-centeredness caused them not to see the needs of the children who were placed in their care. Instead of providing the children with the love and care they deserved, my former foster mother would collect different beating apparatus for the purpose of inflicting physical and psychological pain and suffering on the children. She would stockpile sticks, leather straps, and pieces of garden hose, just for the purpose of beating us.

As I reflect on this experience, it causes me to wonder what my former foster mother's state of mind was when she decided to add the second, third, fourth, fifth, sixth, seventh, and $n^{th}$ stick, piece of garden hose, and custom-made leather strap to her collection. What was her mental state throughout such a process? What could have caused a person to conceive and to follow through with such actions? What was her rationale when it was evident that any one of those devices was more than adequate to harm a child? Why was she always in need of more of the very things that had no purpose other than to bring about physical and psychological harm to a child? And in her quest, she would ensure that the next one had the potential to be more lethal than the ones she already had. I am not sure if she was hoping the sight of those devices would serve as deterrent and she had no

## Chapter 18

intention of using them. If that was her hope, then I guess circumstances must have changed.

In addition to my former foster parents' abusive nature, their love for money, and their desire to have more were what seemed to guide their actions. The benefits they derived from the foster children through the use of fear and intimidation overshadowed their ability to think and act compassionately. Although my foster father was not directly responsible for obtaining those devices, I also hold him accountable because he did very little concerning the abuse that was taking place right before his eyes.

It weighs heavy on my heart that after many years of so much suffering, my brother passed away, never having the opportunity to experience the love and compassion he must have yearned for his entire life. I truly regret that my brother and I were never reunited to share a moment of joy and laughter together. Although I was not able to bring him "back to himself," as he had pleaded with me to do, and my efforts to remove him from the streets did not materialize, I also have to accept the fact that I was unable to control his destiny. I know that it is easy for us to insist that those of us who have been wronged should just "get over it." Or that the afflicted should be patient because time will eventually erase the injustices that were done. However, I am here to remind us that those words are much easier to repeat when we are not the person being wronged or the person being persecuted.

Before I proceed to my closing summary, I would like to make an important and fervent plea as it relates to fostering. It was not until I had an opportunity to reflect on the love and compassion that was bestowed on me by my second foster mother, Aunt Lucy, that I finally realized

*The Afflicted*

that fostering a child should be about *love* and *compassion*, and *NOT* for the convenience of the foster parents. Had it not been for Aunt Lucy, I would most likely have thought my former foster parents' selfish actions were normal and maybe even acceptable. This is why I would like to say that it is not moral, ethical, or humane for anyone to adopt, foster, or become the legal guardian of a child with the intention of that child's becoming his or her housemaid, domestic helper, or servant. No one should use the foster care system as a disguise to fulfill his or her selfish desires! The decision to adopt, foster, or become the legal guardian of a child should *NOT* be motivated by how much economic value the prospective parents can extract from the child or the system. I have witnessed the suffering of the innocent children who found themselves at the mercy of my former foster parents, whose financial interests were far more important to them than the well-being of the children. I have suffered the loss of my only brother to such deceptive monetary greed.

Perhaps these actions were remnants of the slavery mentality that lasted so long under colonial rule in Jamaica. Unsatisfied greed and disregard for human lives are despicable traits that contribute to the exploitation of people, especially minors. And, sadly, it is evident that many such individuals, including my former foster parents, have professed to be God-fearing Christians. I am not sure if they were ignorant or just too arrogant to understand that what they were doing was wrong on all levels! My message is this: If you know of, or have heard of, someone who is considering adopting, fostering, or becoming the legal guardian of a child, please remind him, her, or them that the well-being of a child should *NOT* be used

Chapter 18

as another "to be checked off item" on our social gratification checklist. The love and affection that is yearned for by a child should not be considered or be treated as a social checkbox accomplishment.

## CONCLUSION

# HOW DID I GET HERE?

Throughout my childhood years, I found myself being torn between the Rastafarian doctrine and societal norms. For the first seven years of my childhood, my father introduced me to the Rastafarian doctrine and the need for me to adhere to its principles. Shortly after my seventh birthday, the authorities removed me from my father's care. They transferred me to an orphanage where my life was radically transformed. While at the orphanage, I was forced to conform to a new norm that include different religious beliefs.

After enduring several months of transformation, I was transferred back to my father's care, where I was reintroduced to the Rastafarian doctrine. After approximately a year, the authorities removed me from my father's care and transferred me back to the orphanage. Once again, I had to conform to societal norms.

After residing at the orphanage for several months, at approximately nine years old, I was then transferred to my mother's care. This was the first time that I could remember witnessing my mother. However, due to extreme poverty, my life was all about survival and had little or nothing to do with societal norms, including Christianity

## Chapter 20

and Rastafarianism. After approximately a year of living with my mother, the authorities removed me from her care. They returned me to the orphanage because my basic social and biological needs were not being met.

After living at the orphanage for several months, the authorities transferred me to a foster home. Throughout such times, my foster parents treated me as though my life were insignificant and had no value, except to enrich them them. After enduring a little over five years of constant physical and psychological abuse, I decided to confront them regarding their injustice. Instead of acknowledging their wrongs and changing accordingly, they removed me from their care and returned me to the Child Development Agency. From there, I was placed in a temporary foster home.

It was throughout those years of great upheaval that I truly felt as though all hope had been lost and that my life had no value. However, my hope was restored when the Lord provided for me a wonderful foster parent, Aunt Lucy, who intervened and supported me in every way possible. She removed my fears and elevated my hopes and dreams so that I could realize that my life should be valued. She gave me the courage and determination to persevere against all the odds. Her love and compassion opened my eyes and my understanding to realize the true meaning of fostering.

Irrespective of the unfortunate circumstances that occurred throughout my childhood and adolescent years, I believe that they have taught me the following:

- Being torn between ideologies and religious doctrines has helped me to identify with individuals who are caught between the perceived norms and the religious and social ideologies of society.

## My Beliefs and Philosophy

- Being separated from my parents and placed in an orphanage and foster homes has helped me to understand and to relate to the unfortunate children who have been abandoned or forcibly removed from their parents' care, with little or no regard for the physical and psychological harm that is being done in the process.
- Experiencing extreme poverty, which includes homelessness and hunger, has helped me to understand and to sympathize with those who find themselves at the lowest tier of society.
- Having my hopes and dreams crushed by the very people who had promised to be my wonderful and loving foster parents has helped me to understand and to sympathize with others, especially innocent children whose hopes and dreams have been trampled on by those who have been entrusted to love and care for them.
- Having lost my only brother because he spoke out against injustice has helped me to understand and to relate to any person, especially a child, who has been silenced and stripped of his or her dignity and God-given rights by those who seek to oppress and exploit the less fortunate.

In closing, my life lessons have taught me that life should not always be about, "What is in it for me?" Instead, life should be more about, "What contributions have I made that will be of benefit to others, particularly the less fortunate children?"

∼

Thank you for choosing to read my autobiography, and may the divine principles of life guide you as you strive to make a positive impact on your life and the lives of others.

∼

The Family of a Life Time

# UNITED STATES OF AMERICA - THE JOURNEY

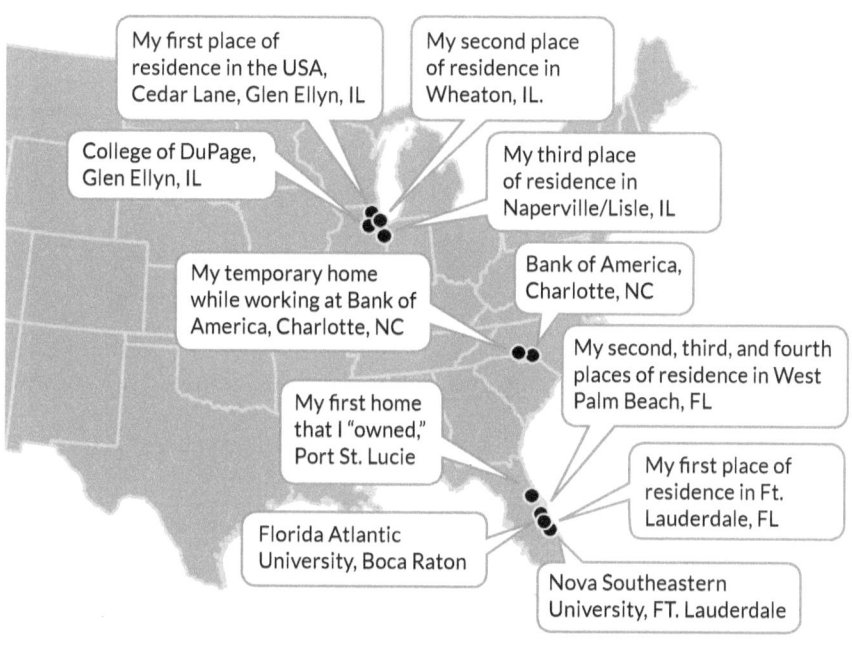

# APPENDIX A

# THE EMOTIONAL AND PSYCHOLOGICAL EFFECT

## A

### INTRODUCTORY PERIOD PERFORMANCE REVIEW FORM

| Employee Name | Job Title | | Hire Date |
|---|---|---|---|
| Desmond Tomlinson | Business Intelligence Analyst | | 9/15/2008 |
| Department | Location | | Date of Review |
| IT – Business Intelligence | | | 1/16/2009 |
| Supervisor Name | Supervisor Title | | |
| | Director, Business Intelligence & E-Business | | |

**KEY PERFORMANCE FACTORS** – Each factor below is accompanied by typical behaviors that reflect performance in that area. Evaluate the employee on those factors that are relevant to his/her job with a rating of either Meets Expectations (ME) or Needs Improvement (NI). Document any factor rated NI, using specific examples whenever possible. Each data block will expand to accommodate any length of text.

| Performance Factor | Comments | ME | NI |
|---|---|---|---|
| 1. **Work Quality**<br>• Completes assignments in a thorough, neat, and accurate manner.<br>• Frequency and magnitude of errors are acceptable given experience and training.<br>• Produces reliable results consistent with job requirements and applicable work procedures. | The quality of work is lacking. Desmond has difficulty in with his communication skills, both verbal and written. | | X |
| 2. **Productivity**<br>• Amount and timeliness of work output is reasonable given experience and training.<br>• Makes effective use of available work time. Meets deadlines. | Tasks go on indefinitely. Assessing a basic BI tool (JasperSoft) has taken substantially longer than necessary. The same is true for coming up to speed with Cognos BI. | | X |
| 3. **Job Knowledge and Skills**<br>• Demonstrates a reasonable level of job knowledge given experience and training.<br>• Able to learn new job skills and integrate them into work processes. | Desmond has difficulty with BI toolsets and does not pick up on new concepts quickly. | | X |
| 4. **Initiative**<br>• Demonstrates willingness to learn the job and produce results.<br>• Shows resourcefulness to find materials, solutions, and guidance/direction to get things done.<br>• Works proactively to accomplish assignments, solve problems, and assist others.<br>• Accepts responsibility for outcomes and final results. | | | X |
| 5. **Teamwork/Interpersonal Skills**<br>• Works effectively and cooperatively with others.<br>• Responds well to situations requiring cooperation, tact, and diplomacy.<br>• Earns acceptance and builds credibility at all levels.<br>• Manages conflict situations to achieve win-win outcomes. | Although Desmond is polite, he depends too heavily on others to help him with his projects. He has not established the level of confidence, his or his peers, to effectively design and implement BI solutions. | | X |
| 6. **Adherence to Company Policies**<br>• Understands and adheres to company policies regarding attendance, work schedules, rules of conduct, use of Company property, safety, cGMP, and other regulatory requirements. | Desmond has not compromised any company policies to my knowledge. | X | |

12-11-02 rev 1

*Appendix A*

**Introductory Period Performance Review Form**
Page 2 of 2

| Employee Name | | Job Title | |
|---|---|---|---|

**7. Resource Management and Leadership (Management Only)**
- Controls operating costs by allocating financial and human resources to achieve goals in the most cost effective way.
- Works effectively with subordinates by setting goals, delegating appropriately, providing performance feedback, coaching, and creating a team-oriented, productive work environment.

**KEY RESULTS / STRENGTHS** – Indicate 3-5 areas in which the employee has demonstrated strong performance.

**DEVELOPMENT NEEDS** – Indicate 3-5 areas that need additional development to improve effectiveness and performance in the current job or to prepare the employee for future career opportunities.

1. Communication skills, especially written, are significantly deficient.
2. Technical depth in BI tools, operating systems and database systems is very week.
3. Problem solving skills are very week.

**ACTION PLAN** – Describe the actions that the employee should take to address his or her development needs. Include timeframes for completion and any coaching and assistance to be provided.

| Action | Who Responsible | Target Completion Date |
|---|---|---|
| | | |
| | | |
| | | |

**PERFORMANCE PLANNING** – If you have not done so already, set key performance objectives for the employee for the coming review period (exempt and nonexempt only). Document these objectives in Section I of the Performance Review Form.

**OVERALL RATING** – Indicate the employee's overall performance during the introductory period and your recommendation for his or her continued employment by checking one box in each section below.

| | Progress Rating | | Recommendation |
|---|---|---|---|
| | Meets or exceeds expectations in most key areas of responsibility | | Satisfactory completion of introductory period |
| | Needs improvement in several key areas of responsibility | | Extend introductory period by _____ days |
| X | Performance does not meet minimal expectations | | Not suited for position – recommend termination |

Nothing in this document changes the at-will nature of any employee's employment, and _____ may terminate or otherwise modify the employment relationship at any time, with or without notice and with or without cause.

Sign the form and submit it to the next level manager and Human Resources for approval prior to your discussion with the employee. The employee should sign following the performance appraisal discussion. The employee's signature indicates that the review was discussed. It does not necessarily imply agreement. Make copies of the form for your files and for the employee, and return the original to HR for placement in the employee's personnel file.

# REFERENCE

Reynolds, Ras Dennis Jabari. *Jabari Authentic Jamaican Dictionary of the Jamic Language Featuring, Jamaican Patwa and Rasta Iyaric, Pronunciations and Definitions.* Around the Way Books, 2006.

www.ingramcontent.com/pod-product-compliance
Lightning Source LLC
Chambersburg PA
CBHW021054080526
44587CB00010B/246